HOW TO WIN OVER WORRY

JOHN EDMUND
HAGGAI

HARVEST HOUSE PUBLISHERS

EUGENE, OREGON

HOW TO WIN OVER WORRY
Copyright © 2001/2009 by John Edmund Haggai
Published by Harvest House Publishers
Eugene, Oregon 97402
www.harvesthousepublishers.com

ISBN 978-0-7369-2627-0

The Library of Congress has cataloged the edition as follows:

Haggai, John Edmund.
    How to win over worry / John Edmund Haggai.—Updated.
        p. cm.
    ISBN 978-0-7369-1753-7
    1. Worry—Religious aspects—Christianity. 2. Christian life. I. Title.
BV4908.5.H3 2001
248.4—dc21   00-053913

09 10 11 12 13 14 15 16 17 / DP-NI / 10 9 8 7 6 5 4 3 2 1

To Christine, my wife of 64 years.

CONTENTS

PREFACE

In the 1950s I began to deliver an address entitled "How to Win Over Worry."

No matter where I spoke, large audiences flowed in. It became clear that I had touched upon a felt need. Thousands of people who attended these meetings requested a copy of the speech.

In 1958, my wife and my associate suggested I reduce the address to print. I set aside three weeks to accomplish this. By the end of 1958 I had finished a 200-page book devoted exclusively to worry. In May the following year, the first copies of *How to Win Over Worry* appeared in bookstores across America.

It was the first of this genre published by a Christian publishing house and released in Christian bookstores. The publisher showed great courage in promoting it. He intended, as I later found out, to let it run for a year or so, then remainder it and let it go out of print.

How *Worry* became a bestseller

Two developments kept the book alive.

One of the publisher's sales representatives announced to Oregon bookstore owner Bob Hawkins, Sr. the publisher's intention to discontinue the book after the present edition was exhausted.

Bob Hawkins owned two bookstores in the state at that time. He said, "That book cannot go out of print." To prove his point, he ordered 500 hardback copies. Purchasing 500 hardback copies for two modest-sized bookstores in a modest-sized city seemed foolhardy. Bob sold all of the books within two months.

In the meantime, I had spoken to Mr. Ellison, who had paperback book concessions in 92 of America's leading airports. Ellison requested the book be put in paperback so he could sell it in the airports. The book sold well.

What Bob Hawkins did for this book and Ellison did for its paperback edition gave it a permanent presence. Had I known of the publisher's plan in 1959 not to reprint the book, I'm sure I never would have written another.

Since Bob's purchase of those 500 copies, it has been translated into 19 languages, gone through more than 50 printings, and sold more than 2,000,000 copies. It has touched the lives of readers in more than 150 countries.

I am delighted that Harvest House, founded by Bob Hawkins, Sr. and now headed by his son Bob Hawkins, Jr., is publishing this new fiftieth anniversary edition.

A remarkable story about *Win Over Worry*

I am now well into the ninth decade of life.

For more than 60 years, I have been before the public on every continent and in scores of nations. I have completed more than 100 trips around the world, and countless international trips.

In all that time, I have found that human nature does not change. In fact, the number of people needing help with worry seems to have increased alarmingly.

South African Andre Petersie, who became a top executive with one of Hollywood's leading film companies, phoned me one day to request that I send the book to a friend of his, a leading impresario in the United Kingdom.

In less than a week after I had sent the book, I received a phone call from London. The name meant nothing to me until I realized this was the man that Petersie asked me to help.

The impresario said, "I want to thank you for the book. I was in the bedroom of my London residence, gun in hand, ready to blow out my brains when I heard a thud downstairs. I looked over the balcony railing to see that a parcel had been put through the mail slot. Curiosity drove me to find out what was in the parcel before I ended my life. It was your book. As a result, my life has been transformed. I have turned it over completely to the Lord Jesus Christ, and I want to thank you for being the instrument to save me not only physically, but also spiritually."

What can reading this book achieve?

This book makes no claim to deal with psychiatric and medical problems. What it does is present a formula for assisting people who are afflicted with anxiety, but who do not suffer from the kind of mental illness that requires professional medical intervention.

After the fifth edition of this book was released, I addressed the Texas Medical Association and found that more than 100 of the doctors were using the book for mildly disturbed patients. Hundreds of clergymen and counselors, both in the United States and overseas, have used the book to help those coming to them for assistance.

I believe that worry is an underlying condition of American society—and probably global society also. Not everyone suffers from clinical depression or psychosis. But everyone, at some time, will worry. And many will find that uncontrolled worry corrodes the joy of living and brings about a deterioration of mind and body.

Of course it is naïve to expect that reading one book once will ever, by itself, produce a total life-change. An outstanding Memphis soprano soloist who read *How to Win Over Worry* told me, "I have read your book, and I am still worrying."

I said, "Ruth, I know you are not too touchy about your age, so tell me how old you are."

Perplexed, she said, "Fifty-three. Why?"

"Am I to conclude that you have been worrying for most of your 53 years?"

"Yes, I have."

"Isn't it illogical to think that, with one reading of a book, you can override 53 years of habit?"

I hold out little hope for anybody who reads the book just once. I myself reread it periodically to reinforce the truths that I need for my own emotional health and vitality—and I am the author!

Just days ago, while putting the final editing touches on this edition, a multinational multibillionaire, whose name is known globally, ordered a copy to read.

Apparently this twenty-first-century "man for all seasons" takes winning over worry seriously.

I suggest you read the book and reread it. Make notes in the margins or inside the back cover about passages that have special relevance to your need. And write out specific goals.

The New York psychiatrist Ari Kiev discovered that patients who set goals and worked toward their fulfillment did much better than those who did not. Goals that are specific and time-sensitive, and broken down into action steps, will give you a real sense of control over your problem and help you climb out of it.

Finally, you will see very soon that the advice this book offers is distilled from another far greater book—the Bible.

When I was a young man, I heard a clinical psychologist say, "What you think about the first five minutes after you awaken will determine the kind of day you have."

I cannot recommend strongly enough that anyone surrounded by worry make time every morning to read the only truly life-changing book that has ever been written.

Immersing yourself in the Holy Bible will improve your upcoming day.

PART 1

WHY YOU CAN WIN

1

WINNERS
AND WORRIERS

In 1969, I stood on the brink of financial disaster.

Just a few years earlier, I'd been the highest-paid church leader in America. God had blessed me with an income level enjoyed by very few in Christian service. At the peak, I'd earned $12,200 in a single month. That equates to $86,800 in 2009 dollars.

And then I'd burned it up.

In pursuit of my God-given vision, I'd sunk every available dollar into an ambitious global training venture that even some of my best friends dismissed as folly. In addition, my wife Christine and I were caring for our invalid son Johnny at a cost of more than $10,000 per year.

With a severely depleted income, I'd cashed in my insurance policies, decimated my savings, and gone deep into debt. I'd just sold my car. If I didn't meet my next mortgage payment, I'd lose the house.

What occurred next forced me to make one of the toughest decisions I've ever made.

I received a call from Dr. Wendell Philips.

As a young man, Philips had led a series of daring exploits in the Middle East that would later inspire the Hollywood character Indiana Jones. At the age of 26 he had set off to find the remains of the

Queen of Sheba's palace, and ended up in a dramatic showdown with the local Yemeni warlords.

Now, a couple of decades later, his extensive work in the Middle East had made him the world's largest independent oil concessionaire. He'd heard of my own roots in the Middle East, on my father's side. He had a proposal to make.

"I want you to work with me for 12 months," he said. "I'll pay you one million dollars upon signing our contract. In addition I'll split the ORRI [overriding royalty interest] with you on any oil discoveries."

By any measurement, this was a fabulous offer. As it turned out, a huge discovery would shortly be made in North Africa, yielding $37 million under the terms of Philips' contract.

But for me, it came at a price.

I sat at my desk and contemplated a future filled with Wendell Philips' money—and a God-given vision that would almost certainly die if I stepped aside at this crucial moment to rescue my finances.

I knew I had no choice.

"I'm sorry," I told him. "I can't do it."

He sounded stunned.

"What's the matter, not enough money?"

"No," I replied. "Your job is too small."

I hung up the phone, wondering what kind of an idiot I was to turn down the chance of more-or-less instant wealth.

I kept hearing the words of the apostle: "If one does not provide for his family, he has denied the faith and is worse than an infidel" (see 1 Timothy 5:8). What was I thinking of?

But I knew I'd done the right thing.

Instead of jetting off to the Middle East with a million dollars in my bank account, I scrambled to ensure that a small group of Christian leaders from around the world could fly to Switzerland and take part in a training program nobody had ever heard of—the program that later became Haggai Institute.

The financial trauma rolled on. Unwilling to subject my wife to additional stress, I kept the money problems strictly to myself. In the end, it took me 22 years to get out of personal debt.

But here's the point: Through all of those years, I could have worried myself to death. Stress could have kept me awake into the early hours. I could have lost my nerve and broken out in a cold sweat as I grappled with a hundred uncertainties. And no one would have blamed me for it.

But I didn't.

Long before my financial crisis hit, I'd learned how to win over worry. I knew that I could choose to worry, or choose *not* to worry. It was my choice. And I preferred winning over worry to having worry win over me.

What have you chosen to worry about?

I can remember exactly when I stopped worrying.

I was 24, a conscientious and hard-working young pastor. I pushed myself so hard that eventually I suffered a nervous breakdown. My doctor ordered me to take time off, and during this enforced convalescence I experienced a 180-degree transformation in my thinking.

With gratitude to God, I can say that, since the fall of 1948, I have not lost five minutes' sleep over any problem, difficulty, tension, or adverse circumstance.

Not that my life has been especially easy. For well over 80 years I've had a pretty generous helping of pressure, uncertainty, and even criticism. That just goes with the territory.

Nor would those who know me say I walk around in a state of unnatural elation. For me, winning over worry has little to do with my emotions. It's a matter of the will—as rational as selecting which restaurant you will go to for dinner.

Looking at the economic events that surround us as I revise this book, I am forced to conclude that most Americans have let worry get out of control. For example, the *Survey of Affluence and Wealth in America* released in May 2009 by the American Express Publishing and

Harrison Group showed that more than half of America's wealthy were worried they could run out of money. According to the same report, four out of five wealthy families felt they have taken a substantial hit to their financial security.

These, in the main, are people who are in no serious danger of becoming poor. But that's how worry works. The radar of worry sweeps far beyond the actual dangers, and makes you believe that you're hemmed in on every side by problems you can't solve.

Winning over worry begins with gaining proper perspective. Every stage of life presents you with things to worry about:

- *Growing up is worrying.* Children and young people often suffer night terrors, exam pressure, bullying, social rejection, and dating stress. Add to that the anxiety resulting from marriage breakdowns and the fear that you might disappoint your parents.

- *Work is worrying.* Most workplaces impose stress. Particularly high on the worry scale are air traffic controllers, CEOs, commodity brokers, workers in the emergency services, local government officials, social service representatives, shift workers, people in sales and tele-sales, teachers, and doctors.

- *Being a woman is worrying.* Women seem inclined toward being emotional burden-bearers. If you're a woman, you will have a natural tendency to worry about your family responsibilities. And if you work and have a family, you may feel guilty about leaving your children when you go to work. Having the man in your life tell you, "Don't worry" usually won't help.

- *Being a parent is worrying.* More than ever before, parents worry about bad things endangering their children. Accidents, assault, using drugs, falling under bad influences. And that's on top of all the normal anxieties about kids achieving adequate grades and finding a good job after they finish school.

- *Past experiences are worrying.* Traumatic experiences leave scars. Suffer abandonment, and you will tend to worry about being abandoned again. Similarly, large numbers of combat troops suffer from PTSD—post traumatic stress disorder.
- *Getting older is worrying.* Older people easily turn into worriers. They feel less in control of life, and more uncertain about the future.

Whichever stage of life you're in, and whatever your situation, you will face challenges. You may lose your job. You may see your children leave home. You may experience deteriorating health. These changes will have an impact on your life. And you can counter that impact, and even capitalize on it, by taking appropriate action.

But worry tries to move all of this out of the zone of *action* and into the zone of *feelings.*

Instead of responding positively and constructively, you begin to...

- sink into self-pity.
- fear that things can only get worse.
- regret past actions that now seem ill-advised.
- wish you had done things differently.
- ask why God "let this happen to you."
- feel angry and resentful that things have gone wrong.
- take a pessimistic view of everything.
- lose your ability to enjoy life.
- worry that you're worrying too much.

Once worry gets a grip, you will soon start worrying about things that don't exist and that aren't materializing.

Many psychologists distinguish two forms of worry: so-called *productive worry* that motivates you to solve your problems, and *destructive worry* that leads to constant anxiety and fear. But categorizing worry in this way makes a false assumption. It asserts that worry is inevitable. Faced with stress, these psychologists claim you will worry, whether you want to or not. So the only question is whether you worry *too much.* In reality, productive worry simply doesn't exist. All worry is destructive. No matter now much stress you're under, *you don't need to worry at all.*

If worry afflicts you, you shouldn't try to analyze how you slid across the line from worrying productively to worrying destructively. You will never find such a line, and agonizing over it will get you nowhere.

It all comes down to this: You choose to worry, or you choose not to.

What happens when you worry

A trained psychologist in the ministry, the recently deceased Dr. Eddie Lieberman, once had to help a young woman who'd become paralyzed.

He went to see her. She told him she was sick, that she didn't love her husband anymore (he was overseas in the armed forces at the time), and that she wanted a divorce. Her physical state was deteriorating badly.

Eddie's instincts as a psychologist told him something was drastically wrong with this woman. He requested permission to admit her to Duke University Hospital. There the true story came out.

Her problems had begun with a letter from her husband. He said he'd fallen in love with another woman. It was he, not she, who wanted to initiate divorce proceedings. Her severe, untreated anxiety had produced the physical symptoms of paralysis.

Eddie Lieberman tried to help her, but she was so deeply mired in the breakdown of her marriage that she had no will to be helped. She should have been a lively, vivacious woman in her mid-thirties. Instead she was a morose paralytic bound for a premature grave. The culprit: worry.

When worry gets out of control, bad things result. You start to experience physical and mental symptoms such as the following:

- painful uneasiness of mind
- muscular tension and headaches
- difficulty in taking a "realistic" view
- restlessness and irritability
- palpitations, sweating, trembling, and nausea
- excessive tiredness
- inability to fall asleep

Awareness of unresolved worry drains the joy from your life. It erodes your confidence and interferes with your personal relationships. The quality of your work suffers. You feel down, unhappy, distracted, frustrated. You lose your vitality. Your posture sags. Worry can fasten its grip on you in the form of physical and mental deterioration.

Why do CEOs suffer the highest incidence of death from heart disease, duodenal ulcers, suicide, and strokes? Worry is a major culprit. As one leading medical doctor put it, "Business people who don't know how to fight worry die young."

Experts agree on the ties that link worry to heart disease, hypertension, and cancer. But it doesn't stop there.

Susan Barr and Jerilynn Prior of the University of British Columbia in Vancouver, Canada, questioned 51 healthy preteen girls about weight worries. They also measured the mineral content of the girls' bones using low-dose X-rays. They were surprised to find that worry over weight linked directly to bone density. The greater the worry, the greater the likelihood that bone density would decline, boosting the risk of osteoporosis.

Worry is an insidious and deadly enemy. It makes you miserable. It makes you sick. And unless you take action, it will become a prison from which you cannot escape.

2

WHERE TO GET HELP

The first question many people ask when they start worrying is, "Do I need to see a doctor?"

Worry *may* be a sign that you have an underlying condition that needs some form of medical intervention (for example, psychosis, bipolar syndrome, manic depression, or clinical depression). And some kinds of worry *may* have deep roots that you can treat more easily with the help of a trained counselor or psychiatrist.

But *most* people who worry—and this includes many who have given their symptoms medical labels such as neurosis, depression, and panic attack—do so simply as a result of struggling unsuccessfully with the pains and pressures life throws at them.

As you would expect, a multimillion dollar industry has grown up to help them cope. Go on the Internet and you'll find an astonishing range of psychiatric therapies. Go to the drugstore and you'll find countless pharmaceutical products, including many types of antidepressants.

Consider what these solutions tell you.

A psychiatrist is a kind of mind mechanic. When you consult a psychiatrist, you are saying there is something wrong with your mind, some hidden flaw or contradiction, that the psychiatrist can uncover and fix—or at least help to treat.

A pharmaceutical product is a chemical. When you take it, you are saying you have some kind of metabolic imbalance that you hope can be rectified, or that you wish to suppress that part of your mental function through which you are experiencing anxiety.

After my nervous breakdown at age 24, I rejected both these diagnoses. I did not accept that my mind was in some way damaged or deficient. Nor did I accept that I could deal with stress by altering my brain chemistry. Instead, I went to the New Testament.

In the Bible, you find a completely different analysis of worry and a completely different solution to it.

New Testament Greek scholars correctly translate the Greek verb translated "to worry" with the words, "to take thought," "to be anxious," and "to be careful." And the Greek verb *merimnaō* comes from two words—*merizō,* meaning "to divide," and *nous,* meaning "mind" (a term that refers to the faculties of perceiving, understanding, feeling, judging, and determining).

In the thinking of the New Testament, then, worry implies "a divided mind" lacking unity of thought or action. Part of you tugs in one direction; another part tugs in the other. You are like a trailer with cars pulling at it from each end.

No wonder the apostle James concludes, "a double minded man is unstable in all his ways" (James 1:8). When you worry, you express conflict of purpose. "Unstable" captures the idea accurately. When worry wins, you become unstable in your emotions. Unstable in your thought processes. Unstable in your decisions. Unstable in your judgments.

- Worry divides your *feelings*—causing your emotions to become uneven and volatile.

- Worry divides your *understanding*—making your convictions lose their grounding, sapping you of confidence.

- Worry divides your *perception*—meaning you are distracted and often fail to see the whole situation confronting you.

- Worry divides your *judgment*—making your decision-making ill informed and unreliable.

- Worry divides your *will*—producing lethargy and dulling your ability to pursue your goals with confidence.

Worry causes heartbreak, failure, misunderstanding, suspicion, relationship breakdown, and much unhappiness. Left long enough, this division of the mind becomes so severe that you can no longer muster the energy to struggle against your problems. You go through a nervous breakdown, or develop the symptoms of a more severe mental disorder.

Do you have a divided mind?

Look at the kinds of personal problems that cause people worry. It's not long before you can see the divided mind behind it.

For example, marital breakdown reveals a loss of single-minded devotion to a relationship. The husband's affections may become divided between his wife and another woman. It may be that a wife's loyalty is divided between her husband and her mother. A parent's will and attention can be divided between responsibilities to children and responsibilities to the spouse. A wage earner may divide his or her mind between the needs of family and the driving ambition to succeed in a career.

A divided mind can afflict children. I grew up in a preacher's home, and I know how intense the pressures can be. If you are a "model child," you get held up by other parents as a pattern for their own kids to emulate—with the result that the other kids detest you. On the other hand, if you give in to your natural bent for mischief, you win the approval of your friends, but the wrath of your parents.

I have a brother who was so sensitive about being a preacher's son that he deliberately got poor grades in school so his friends wouldn't think of him as a "goody-goody." He had an excellent mind—a fact later proved by his collegiate scholastic records. In the end he graduated with honors in electrical engineering at one of the nation's leading universities. In 1971, he was given the L.A. Hyland award for scientific achievement. He led the group that produced and launched Syncom Satellite. Much of the work done to produce the detection and communications components of AWACS planes took place in his department under his leadership. But while he was in high school, he let worry ruin his academic performance.

In many cases, the outcomes of worry reveal far greater damage. Barely a day goes by when we don't hear about children failing at school because they have to cope with difficult problems at home. Neglect distracts them from study. Sometimes divorcing parents end up forcing children to make a painful emotional choice. When children sense a lack of care at home, they often create havoc at school. In doing so, they are seeking the attention and affection their family denies them.

Or look at the business world. Only the Lord knows how many businesses have been torpedoed by a divided mind. In the late 1920s, an uneducated European immigrant opened a hot-dog stand. His business grew. Soon he owned a chain of stands. His income soared at a time when unemployment hit 25 percent. He sent his son to a university, where he graduated with a major in business administration. The father proudly brought him into the business.

The son said, "You know, Dad, there's a depression on. Business is bad everywhere. Many businesses have gone into bankruptcy. We must be careful. Let's cut down our inventory, reduce our advertising budget, lay off some of the help, and tighten our belts."

Against his better judgment, the father listened to his "learned" son and followed the advice. Yes, you guessed it. The son succeeded in dividing his father's mind between confidence in the tested principles of success and outright fear of bankruptcy. Soon their business folded. Worse yet, depressed by the financial reverses, the father lost his sparkle, his drive, his optimistic outlook—and began to deteriorate physically.

One of the most bitter and cynical men I have ever known was loaded with talent. He had more ability than six of his peers. He could have been a leading cartoonist, a top-notch photographer, a highly paid after-dinner speaker, a humorist, a prosperous realtor, a topflight hotel executive, or a celebrated writer. But he failed to achieve anything worthwhile, or even earn a decent living. He became an embarrassment to his family and friends.

He saw men without a fraction of his ability soar to the heights of success while he remained a nonachiever. Those who knew and loved him saw that his mind was divided. He never managed to make career choices. He could not say with the apostle Paul, "This one thing I do" (Philippians 3:13). He would never throw all of his energies into a single project. He aimed at nothing, hit a bull's-eye, and then brooded over the result.

What a waste. He became critical of others who did achieve. He rationalized his failure and dealt out misery to his associates. Worry borne of indecision stripped him of his influence, and eventually, of his health.

So what are you going to do about it?

Worry is endemic.

It infiltrates businesses and brings them crashing down. It roars through homes like a tornado, leaving in its wake smashed family relationships—bitter and frustrated parents, and insecure, emotionally damaged children. It drives some to spend fortunes on psychotherapy, and sends others into psychiatric care.

In America, and probably in many other countries as well, worry has virtually become part of the culture. On countless gravestones worldwide, you could write this epitaph:

> *Hurried*
> *Worried*
> *Buried*

Most people who worry may envision a future in which their worries are over. But this remains a dream. The life-transforming events that people think will dispel their cares—for example, winning the lottery—actually force them to exchange one set of worries for another. It's naïve to think that the world around you will suddenly resolve into serene bliss. It's equally naïve to think that a new job or relationship will lift you above your troubles. They won't.

If you're worried now, I can guarantee you'll be worried in five or ten years' time—even if you've become fabulously rich or have married a world-class celebrity. Nothing inside you will change. And why would you expect a different result when, day after day, you just keep on doing the same old thing?

I know from my own experience that there is one—and *only* one—sure answer to worry. But before I get to that, I want to review quickly some other options worriers choose and explain why they never work.

3

SEVEN THINGS
NOT TO TRY

Worry needs a comprehensive and long-term solution. To win, you've got to deal with the problem at its source. Everything else is a waste of your time.

Yet it's amazing how many people will grasp at the nearest and easiest option.

The intimidated choose flattery

You flatter others if you want to keep them from hurting you. So people with fragile egos and who feel weak in the presence of others often use flattery as a means of self-protection.

It functions like a bribe. You tell the other person what you think he or she wants to hear in the hope this will neutralize any potential hostility they harbor toward you and elicit a kind response.

Yet flattery is nothing but a mind game. If the other person really dislikes you, flattery won't keep the hostility at bay for very long. And if there is no hostility, then you are sowing the seeds of your own undoing. How can you secure the lasting good opinion of others by telling them lies?

Insincerity shows. Consequently, someone who might otherwise have thought well of you will be driven into suspicion and resentment. Worry reaps its own reward.

Not surprisingly, the Word of God denounces flattery more than 30 times. Job says: "He that speaketh flattery to his friends, even the eyes of his children shall fail" (Job 17:5). And, "Let me not, I pray you, accept any man's person, neither let me give flattering titles unto man. For I know not to give flattering titles; in so doing my maker would soon take me away" (Job 32:21-22).

The psalmist declares the sinfulness and foolishness of flattery in Psalm 5:9: "There is no faithfulness in their mouth…they flatter with their tongue." Also, "they speak vanity every one with his neighbor; with flattering lips and with a double heart do they speak" (Psalm 12:2).

The wisest man in all history, Solomon, admonishes us: "He that goeth about as a talebearer revealeth secrets: therefore meddle not with him that flattereth with his lips" (Proverbs 20:19). And, "A lying tongue hateth those that are afflicted by it; and a flattering mouth worketh ruin" (Proverbs 26:28).

The resentful start to criticize

Criticizing others seems to take the sting out of worry, at least temporarily.

First, when we criticize, we feel good. We feel as though we're standing on the moral high ground—a position from which everyone else will look up to us.

Second, when we criticize, we project our misery onto others. If everyone else is miserable too, we feel less conspicuous. Also, it takes our mind off our own problems—at least for a short time.

Third, when we criticize, we create the illusion that we have overcome the thing that worries us—by condemning the same thing in someone else.

Of course, criticizing brings only temporary relief. Tragically, criticism further focuses our minds upon negative thoughts, and the mischief that inevitably follows negative thinking only adds to our worries and intensifies our feeling of depression.

The Bible tells us that to the impure, all things are impure (Titus 1:15). Similarly, to the dishonest, all things are dishonest. To the untrue, all things are untrue. When the worrier criticizes others, he solves none of his worries. Instead he focuses his attention upon the miserable traits he sees in others, which mirror his own condition.

Thus riveted to a destructive and negative pattern of thought, he further supplements his already overstocked supply of fears. In addition, criticizing doesn't win approval. As a proverb tells us, "What Peter says about Paul tells more about Peter than it does about Paul."

Another Paul, writing in the New Testament (Romans 2:1), says, "Thou art inexcusable, O man, whosoever thou art that judgest: for wherein thou judgest another, thou condemnest thyself; for thou that judgest doest the same things."

What the worrier fails to realize is that in criticizing others, he reveals to the world the very problem he is trying to conceal.

Those in denial often bury their heads in work

Another useless response to worry is to throw yourself into excessive activity.

Work overpowers the attention; it keeps the mind from straying onto painful thoughts. But work has no power to take pain away. When you finish your shift, or come home from the office, your problems still await you. And unhappily, you now have less, not more, energy to deal with them.

Frenetic activity postpones your appointment with worry. And you won't perform well at work as long as your worries continue to simmer. People who work to hide worry often give the appearance of being busy. Truth is, they don't accomplish much of substance.

An astounding number of people in senior positions work themselves into the ground in an effort to suppress worry. They embody the modern-day beatitude, "Blessed are they who go around in circles, for they shall be called big wheels." But feverish activity, motivated by the desire to escape rather than the urge to produce, solves nothing. It can briefly take the mind off fear-producing thoughts, but in the long term, it only multiplies problems, and thereby intensifies the very condition the worrier wants to solve.

Jesus never associated work with relief from worry. He said to His disciples: "Come ye yourselves apart into a desert place, and rest a while" (Mark 6:31).

The insecure look for sympathy

Another ineffective strategy against worry is to give in to it and present the struggle with it as a sort of heroism. But there is nothing heroic about buckling under to something you see as inevitable. Yet you will hear people speak as though worries were medals won in the heat of battle. They will assert, "My cross is heavy, but I am determined to bear it valiantly." That borders on blasphemy. Wherever the biblical injunction "Take up thy cross" appears, it refers to death to sin and death to self—the exact antithesis of putting up with worry.

The Bible never refers to any problem, grief, or dilemma as a cross, nor does it commend people with worries as though they were called to some special service. The person who *really* bears a cross knows no worry. He has died to sin and to self. Thus he insulates himself from destructive fears. He has peace because his mind is firmly set upon Christ.

Jesus never complained about the weight of His cross. And yet His cross, a real instrument of death and not just a metaphor, imposed a physical suffering none of us could endure with such grace.

Following His example, our Lord's disciples rejoiced that "they were counted worthy to suffer shame for his name" (Acts 5:41). By contrast, people who respond to worry, fear, and anxiety with a self-righteous resignation say one thing but live another. They fool no one but themselves. Although they claim to bring glory to God, their faces show despair and gloom.

Their biblical inspiration isn't Jesus; it is Jonah, sulking outside

Nineveh and saying, "O Lord, take, I beseech thee, my life from me; for it is better for me to die than to live" (Jonah 4:3). Or Elijah, fleeing from Jezebel: "It is enough; now, O Lord, take away my life; for I am not better than my fathers" (1 Kings 19:4). (I always chuckle when I read that passage. If Elijah had stayed in Jezebel's city, she would gladly have granted his petition!)

Don't mistake grumbling for spiritual heroism. Call it by its names: cowardice and unbecoming self-pity. Instead of tackling the problem head on by reforming thought patterns and taking corrective action, the worrier sits down and moans.

The fearful sometimes drift toward substance abuse

Alcohol, cigarettes, and narcotics all lead the worrier into the same dead end. Who can calculate the damage done by the TV dramas and movies that portray the unrequited lover desperately hitting the corner bar to drink away his sorrows? When trouble comes, too many people seek comfort in some form of drug. The idea that a drinking spree opens up an escape hatch has pernicious results. The Japanese say, "A man takes a drink, then the drink takes a drink, and the next drink takes the man."

Solomon, the sage of the ages, speaks wisely when he says, "Who hath woe? who hath sorrow? who hath contentions? who hath babbling? who hath wounds without cause? who hath redness of eyes? They that tarry long at the wine; they that go to seek mixed wine" (Proverbs 23:29-30).

It is still true that, "wine is a mocker, strong drink is raging: and whosoever is deceived thereby is not wise" (Proverbs 20:1). Three millennia later, the only thing that's changed is the variety of chemicals at our disposal. Alcohol now comes in hundreds of different packages. So does nicotine. If these fail, we can obtain any number of more powerful narcotics—legal or otherwise.

They all have the same effect. Temporary exhilaration diverts the mind from fear-producing thoughts. Then the sufferer is unceremoniously dumped back where he or she was at the beginning—in many cases, with the addition of a blinding headache. This pattern of behavior only ignores the problem and ultimately increases the pain.

The determined may try to think positively

Now positive thinking is good, as far as it goes. Certainly a person cannot have positive thoughts and fear-producing thoughts at the same time. The question is whether positive thinking supplies us with the "fuel" we need to move forward. It is one thing to *know* what we ought to do. It is another thing to *have the ability* to do it.

The same dilemma arises with the Old Testament law. The Ten Commandments showed humanity what to be and what to do. But nobody—the Lord Jesus Christ excepted—has ever succeeded in keeping them. People may read the rule book, but they don't live by the rules.

I wholeheartedly believe in the power of positive thinking. Let it be understood, however, that God alone is the source of positive thoughts. Paul says in 2 Timothy 1:7, "God hath not given us the spirit of fear; but of power, and of love, and of a sound mind."

Positive thinking will prove counterfeit if it lures us into thinking that we—in our own strength and by our own resources—can bring about the shift in mental attitude necessary to banish worry. You might just as well try to shoot an African lion with a water pistol as try to conquer worry with a self-inspired and self-produced positive attitude.

Positive thinking needs God. That is why this book refers to it only in the context of a relationship with God. Otherwise, positive thinking is as useless as every other so-called solution to worry.

You will not experience peace unless you are willing to address yourself properly to the Lord Jesus Christ, who is the Prince of Peace. Separated from that divine help, a proper mental attitude cannot be achieved and sustained. Convince yourself that you can beat worry on your own merely by applying the right mental technique, and you will condemn yourself to failure and frustration.

The trapped consider the "easy" way out

One of the most heartrending articles I've ever read appeared on the front page of the May 21, 1931 edition of *The New York Times*. The article was about the suicide of Ralph Barton. He was an outstanding cartoonist, one of the nation's best. He was highly gifted both as an artist and a writer. Yet his life ended tragically by his own hand. In his suicide note he told about the melancholia he had been suffering. Apparently his fears nearly drove him mad.

Part of his note read:

> Melancholia has prevented my getting anything like the full value out of my talent, and the past three years has made work a torture to do at all. It has made it impossible for me to enjoy the simple pleasures of life.

He went on:

> I have run from wife to wife, from house to house, and from country to country, in a ridiculous effort to escape from myself. In doing so I am very much afraid that I have brought a great deal of unhappiness to those who have loved me…No one thing is responsible for this, and no one person but myself…I did it because I am fed up with inventing devices for getting through the twenty-four hours a day and with bridging over a few months periodically with some beautiful interest…

Poor fellow. He was brilliant of mind! How tragic that a life such as his, filled with great possibilities for blessing his generation in the will of God, had to end in such tragedy. The note traces clearly the trail of failed solutions. He could have won over worry, but he never found the way to do it.

The American Association of Suicidology recently drew attention to the link between suicide and the economy—or rather, the lack of a link. Suicide rates have shown no clear association with times of economic recession (the assertion that ruined millionaires jumped from skyscraper ledges in 1929, for example, is mostly myth).

However, a clear relationship exists between suicide and unemployment. In early 2009, suicide hotlines in a number of American states reported significant increases in call volume, prompting warnings from the World Health Organization that many nations could see rises in suicide rates as a result of personal financial tragedy.

Suicide is the last, most desperate, and ultimately most selfish solution to worry. It doesn't do away with worry; it simply transfers it onto the friends and loved ones left behind.

4

THE ANSWER
TO WORRY

Why do we worry?

You may answer that it's human nature. In every age of which we have historical record, people have worried. So who can avoid it?

I've heard people say, "It's just the way I am. My mother was a worrier, and my father was a worrier. So I am a worrier too. It's in the genes."

But try as you may, you cannot blame your worries on a congenital condition—either one contained in your particular genetic make-up or one afflicting the entire human race.

A Democrat from the South asked a man living in Vermont, "Why are you a Republican?"

The Vermonter answered, "My father was a Republican, my grand-father was a Republican, and therefore, I am a Republican."

The Southerner said, "Suppose your father had been a fool and your grandfather had been a fool. Then what would you be?"

"Oh," the man replied, "in that case, I'd be a Democrat."

It doesn't make any more sense to trace worry to your genes than it does to trace your political convictions to your genes. You cannot excuse either one as an uncontrollable state of mind.

According to the Bible, there is a far simpler explanation.

Where worry comes from

If somebody were to walk up to you and point a loaded gun at your chest, your body would react.

Your heart rate would soar. You would start pumping adrenalin. You would break out into a sweat. And your mind would focus sharply on doing whatever you could to prevent your assailant from pulling the trigger.

Those are all natural and largely involuntary responses. God has made you and your body capable of responding to emergencies and going into a state of high readiness and alertness. And of course it doesn't take being robbed at gunpoint to produce this kind of reaction. Every day you face experiences to which your body responds by preparing for action. Sometimes this helps, and sometimes it doesn't.

But worry never achieves anything positive. It solves no crisis.

Worry operates in your mind. Worry is a mental state that allows itself to be dragged along by fear-inducing stimuli. Or it perceives stimuli as fear-inducing when in fact they are not. And it's a mental state to which, actively or passively, you give your consent. At some point, at some level, you have *chosen* to "take your hands off the steering wheel" and given into worry.

Here we confront the heart of the matter. Most worriers will say, "My worry is an affliction. I deserve sympathy." The Bible replies, "Choosing to worry is a sin."

Worry is a sin for three reasons:

Worry is a sin because worriers distrust God

When you worry, you accuse God of falsehood.

God's Word says, "We know that all things work together for good to them that love God, to them who are the called according to his purpose" (Romans 8:28). Yet worry says, "This is not true—God's Word cannot be trusted!"

God's Word says, "He hath done all things well" (Mark 7:37). Yet worry says, "This is not true—God's Word cannot be trusted!"

God's Word says, "I can do all things through Christ which strengtheneth me" (Philippians 4:13). Yet worry says, "This is not true—God's Word cannot be trusted!"

God's Word says, "My God shall supply all your need according to his riches in glory by Christ Jesus" (Philippians 4:19). Yet worry says, "This is not true—God's Word cannot be trusted!"

God's Word says, "I will never leave thee, nor forsake thee" (Hebrews 13:5). Yet worry says, "This is not true—God's Word cannot be trusted!"

God's Word says, "He careth for you" (1 Peter 5:7). Yet worry says, "This is not true—God's Word cannot be trusted!"

God's Word says, "Take no thought for your life, what ye shall eat, or what ye shall drink; nor yet for your body, what ye shall put on...for your heavenly Father knoweth that ye have need of all these things" (Matthew 6:25,32). Yet worry says, "This is not true—God's Word cannot be trusted!"

Worry wears the cloak of hypocrisy, for it professes faith in God and at the same time assails the truth of His promises.

You insult a truthful man when you call him a liar. How infinitely less excusable it is to accuse the sovereign God of falsehood! Scripture asserts that God, by His very nature, cannot deceive. As Christians, we live "in hope of eternal life, which God, that cannot lie, promised before the world began" (Titus 1:2). Consequently, "He that believeth not God hath made him a liar" (1 John 5:10).

Worry is a sin because it damages the temple of God

Imagine a group of vandals crashing into your church some dark night and shattering the windows, ripping up the carpeting, smashing the furniture, wrecking the musical instruments, spraying graffiti on the walls, and ravaging the Sunday school rooms.

What would you do?

Almost certainly, you would react with justifiable anger. If the intruders were caught, you would prosecute them to the full extent of the law, which provides stringent penalties for the destruction of property. Vandalism is costly, wasteful, and destructive, and we are right to condemn it.

But compare this vandalizing of a church building with what anxiety does to your bodily health. In all probability, the vandals were not professing Christians. Yet many worriers are. Furthermore, there is no eternal value in a church building. True, it symbolizes worship. It symbolizes the work and the Word of God. But the people of God do not suffer injury if a church building is destroyed. God does not dwell in the sanctuary; He dwells in the hearts of those who worship there.

> *1 Corinthians 3:16*—"Know ye not that ye are the temple of God, and that the Spirit of God dwelleth in you?"

> *1 Corinthians 6:19*—"What? Know ye not that your body is the temple of the Holy Ghost which is in you, which ye have of God, and ye are not your own?"

> *1 Peter 2:5*—"Ye also, as lively stones, are built up a spiritual house, an holy priesthood, to offer up spiritual sacrifices, acceptable to God by Jesus Christ."

> *Galatians 4:6*—"Because ye are sons, God hath sent forth the Spirit of his Son into your hearts."

If you are a Christian, remember that worry damages and even destroys the temple of God, which is your body.

In the first chapter I mentioned the now well-established link between worry and disease. Consider again the vast range of ways in which worry affects your physical and mental well-being: Anxiety produces heart trouble, high blood pressure, asthma, rheumatism, ulcers and other stomach disorders, colds, thyroid malfunction, arthritis, migraine headaches, blindness, palpitations, back and neck pain, indigestion, nausea, constipation, diarrhea, dizziness, fatigue, insomnia, allergies, and more.

In short, worry damages your body more severely than any vandals could damage a church.

Worry is a sin because it damages relationships

When you worry, it's not only your body that suffers. In all kinds of ways, worry infects and degrades your ability to relate to others.

1. Worry damages your relationship with God.

Worry is a sin because it is symptomatic of prayerlessness. "Moreover as for me, God forbid that I should sin against the LORD in ceasing to pray for you" (1 Samuel 12:23).

No one can pray and worry at the same time, as God tells Isaiah: "Thou wilt keep him in perfect peace, whose mind is stayed on thee: because he trusteth in thee" (Isaiah 26:3). When you pray, your mind is set on Christ, and you have His assurance of perfect peace. Worry is therefore banished.

2. Worry damages your relationship with your family.

Paul wrote to the Ephesians, "Wives, submit yourselves unto your own husbands, as unto the Lord…Husbands, love your wives, even as Christ also loved the church, and gave himself for it…Nevertheless let every one of you in particular so love his wife even as himself; and the wife see that she reverence her husband" (Ephesians 5:22,25,33). These injunctions in the book of Ephesians are violated and disobeyed when worry sits in the saddle.

3. Worry damages your relationship with unbelievers.

Did you know worry undermines your Christian witness? In Matthew 5:16 Jesus says, "Let your light so shine before men, that they may see your good works, and glorify your Father which is in heaven." Who would want to join a church full of worriers?

Someone may say, "Oh, yes, Dr. Haggai, it's all very well for you to talk like that in an overly confident and pedantic manner. After all, you are an ordained minister. What do you know about worry?"

Well, let me remind you of where I started. I too hold the distinction of having suffered a so-called nervous breakdown. I say so-called because we are mistaken if we see such crises as originating in the nervous system. Most breakdowns are not organic in nature; rather, they spring directly from pressure of circumstance. They arise when we allow our lives to tumble out of control.

By emphasizing that worry is a sin, I don't mean that you should add "God is angry with me" to your list of things to worry about. Rather, I simply want to point out that understanding the sinful nature of worry will set you free. Why? Because you will no longer see worry as an affliction you can do nothing about. Usually we have no control over whether we become ill. But we *can* control whether we worry. Illnesses often require external help, whereas worry requires internal repentance.

You may ask whether repenting of worry will really make a difference.

When I was 20 years old, I was involved in a four-car accident. Litigation proceedings began almost immediately. I needed help desperately. I needed the resources of the greatest accident lawyer in the country. His name was Weinstein, and his fee was understandably large. So large that I, as a ministerial student, could not meet it. However, a dear friend came to see me. He was the owner of a large company in Chicago. He said, "Haggai, Weinstein is our lawyer. We retain him. Here, let me give you one of my cards."

On the back of the card my friend scribbled a note of introduction to Weinstein. As a result, Weinstein saw me. He solved my legal problem. Why? Because of a fee I paid? Not at all. He saw me because of the fee paid by my friend.

The Lord Jesus Christ is the Friend "that sticketh closer than a brother" (see Proverbs 18:24). He paid the fee that I could not pay—the fee for the penalty of sin. He paid it with His own blood. In His name and on His merits I have access to God, who alone can solve my problems.

You must begin, then, by consciously turning around, consciously rejecting worry, and consciously pursuing the life God wants you to live.

What the Bible says about worry

While there are many verses of Scripture relevant to worry, two in particular are worthy of reading carefully.

> Rejoice in the Lord alway: and again I say, Rejoice. Let your moderation be known unto all men. The Lord is at hand. Be careful for nothing; but in every thing by prayer and supplication with thanksgiving let your requests be made known unto God. And the peace of God, which passeth all understanding, shall keep your hearts and minds through Christ Jesus. Finally, brethren, whatsoever things are true, whatsoever things are honest, whatsoever things are just, whatsoever things are pure, whatsoever things are lovely, whatsoever things are of good report; if there be any virtue, and if there be any praise, think on these things (Philippians 4:4-8).

J.B. Phillips translates the same passage as follows:

> Delight yourselves in the Lord, yes, find your joy in him at all times. Have a reputation for being reasonable, and never forget the nearness of your Lord. Don't worry over anything whatever; whenever you pray tell God every detail of your needs in thankful prayer, and the peace of God, which surpasses human understanding, will keep constant guard over your hearts and minds as they rest in Christ Jesus. My brothers I need only add this. If you believe in goodness and if you value the approval of God, fix your minds on whatever is true and honorable and just and pure and lovely and admirable (Philippians 4:4-8 PHILLIPS).

Now give thought to the words of our Lord in Matthew 6:25-34:

I tell you, stop being perpetually uneasy (anxious and worried) about your life, what you shall eat or what you shall drink; or about your body, what you shall put on. Is not life greater [in quality] than food, and the body [far above and more excellent] than clothing? Look at the birds of the air; they neither sow nor reap nor gather into barns, and yet your heavenly Father keeps feeding them. Are you not worth more than they? And who of you by worrying and being anxious can add one unit of measure (cubit) to his stature or to the span of his life? [Psalm 39:5-7]. And why should you be anxious about clothes? Consider the lilies of the field and learn thoroughly how they grow; they neither toil nor spin. Yet I tell you, even Solomon in all his magnificence (excellence, dignity, and grace) was not arrayed like one of these [1 Kings 10:4-7]. But if God so clothes the grass of the field, which today is alive and green and tomorrow is tossed into the furnace, will He not much more surely clothe you, O you of little faith?

Therefore do not worry and be anxious, saying, What are we going to have to eat? or, What are we going to have to drink? or, What are we going to have to wear? For the Gentiles (heathen) wish for and crave and diligently seek all these things, and your heavenly Father knows that you need them all. But seek for (aim at and strive after) first of all His kingdom, and His righteousness (His way of doing and being right), and then all these things taken together will be given you besides. So do not worry or be anxious about tomorrow, for tomorrow will have worries and anxieties of its own. Sufficient for each day is its own trouble (AMP).

Practice the nearness of God

I'm going to highlight just one phrase from the above verses: "never forget the nearness of your Lord" (Philippians 4:5 PHILLIPS).

As a child, I was small and sickly and the prey of every bully on the school playground. One day during the summer vacation of 1934, I was in Grand Rapids, Michigan, with my cousin, Alex Haddad. I had accompanied him to Seymour Square to pick up some groceries for his mother. We had nearly returned to their little house on Burton Street when three big fellows in a pickup truck came by and shouted, "Haddad, get yourself and that blankety-blank cousin of yours out of here before we mop up the gutter with you."

Immediately I cringed. I thought to myself, *Uh-oh, here comes another beating.*

Then I looked over at Alex, and my fears subsided; a peaceful calm replaced them. In fact, I started to smile. That year, Alex was the AAU (Amateur Athletic Union) wrestling champion in the 175-pound division. At age 15, he was very much a man. His biceps were like cannonballs and his pectoral muscles were like marble slabs.

Strangely, Alex did not answer back. I said, "Alex, you're not going to let them get away with that, are you?"

"Well, John, you know what the Bible says: If they hit you on one cheek, turn the other."

I had never remembered Alex being that spiritual before, but I was in no position to contest his decision! So I kept walking with him toward the house. We went inside the little picket fence, and just as we got to the front door, he handed the other bag of groceries to me and said, "John, take these in to Mom. Tell her I forgot something; I'll be right back."

I knew exactly what Alex had forgotten. I shoved the groceries inside the front door and trailed him back down to Seymour Square. He surmised that the three roughnecks were on their way to Miller's ice cream parlor. I got there just in time to watch Alex knock the biggest of the three fellows out cold and addle a second fellow with another powerful blow, while the third ran away in stark terror.

I pushed back the shoulders of my four-foot, ten-inch frame, brushed the palms of my hands together, and said to myself, *Anyone else?*

What had converted me from a terrified little boy to a calm and serene fellow brimming with confidence? A simple answer: Alex was near. In the same way, the Lord is near to all who profess faith in Him. "Let your moderation be known unto all men. The Lord is at hand" (Philippians 4:5).

A literal translation of the last part of Philippians 4:5 shows that the verb is missing—"the Lord near." No verb is needed. It is abrupt, staccato. It is a bolt of light. The awareness of God's nearness gives great calm in the storm and stress of life.

Living in the awareness of that fact brings about a behavioral change that cannot be explained in human terms. It's often the only major difference between a defeated Christian and a victorious one. Fortune may have eluded you. Professional success, which you have sought so laboriously, may have slipped through your fingers. Love may have betrayed you. All those may be true.

But the Lord is near! There is no mockery in that statement. Those few words impel us to observe the mandates set down in Philippians 4:4-8.

Understand the nearness of God

Now, what does it mean for the Lord to be "near"? Bible commentators distinguish four kinds of nearness.

1. The Lord is present.

God is near to us at all times. "Thou art near, O Lord," sang the psalmist (Psalm 119:151). And the apostle Paul echoes and glorifies the ancient song. The Lord is near in that He indwells, by the Holy Spirit, the individual Christian. He is "Christ in you" (Colossians 1:27).

2. God is available.

The psalmist cried, "The Lord is nigh unto all them that call upon him" (Psalm 145:18). Here again the New Testament echoes the Old Testament.

As children of God, we have God's ear because we have His heart.

A distant Lord would depress us and distress us. An unapproachable Savior could not help us. Thank God, Christ is approachable. "We have not an high priest which cannot be touched with the feeling of our infirmities; but was in all points tempted like as we are, yet without sin. Let us therefore come boldly unto the throne of grace, that we may obtain mercy, and find grace to help in time of need" (Hebrews 4:15-16).

3. God is compassionate.

The Lord is not indifferent to the trials you go through. The psalmist affirmed this truth when he sang, "The LORD is nigh unto them that are of a broken heart" (Psalm 34:18). Who has not known the distress of a broken heart? "God is…a very present help in trouble" (Psalm 46:1). The awareness of Christ's compassion induces poise.

4. God will return.

The Lord promised He will one day return in the clouds of heaven with great glory. I believe His coming is sooner than we think—the possibility was certainly very real to the early Christians. The Lord Himself declared His future return in unambiguous terms.

Jesus could come at any time. In the silence and darkness of midnight His trumpet may suddenly sound and His awful glory blaze upon us! Our love and anticipation of His appearing is the greatest inducement to obedience. Every command laid upon us is more easily fulfilled when we are motivated by the continuous awareness of the possibility that Jesus may come today. "Be ye also ready" (Matthew 24:44).

Readiness for Christ's return should motivate us toward growth in Christian character and make us more like Him who is our great Exemplar.

The peace formula

I can write hundreds of pages about the nearness of God. But it won't do a bit of good unless you are willing to listen and internalize the truths about His nearness. That is what the rest of this book sets out to do.

The next section contains 21 short chapters. In each one, I will explain how you can replace worry with a definite and focused action. By choosing that action, you choose *not* to worry.

You can sum up those actions in a simple formula for winning over worry:

PRAISE + POISE + PRAYER = PEACE

Why praise, poise, and prayer?

Praise

Living in awareness of the nearness of our Lord will give you strength and the inclination to express praise even when circumstances would drag your spirits down. It will dispel the clouds of pessimism and lead you into the sunshine of enthusiasm and optimism. You cannot live in the consciousness of His nearness and go around looking as if you were born in crab-apple time, put up in vinegar, and weaned on a dill pickle.

Poise

You will find poise much easier to achieve as you live in the consciousness of the nearness of your Lord. For instance, you will find that your thoughts are pleasing to God, and therefore positive—thus putting worry on the run. As you live in the awareness of His nearness, you will realize a strength that is not your own, enabling you to exercise the self-control that leads to establishing poise and banishing worry. "The steps of a good man are ordered by the LORD" (Psalm 37:23).

Prayer

When we pray we don't always feel the nearness of God. In difficult times, God can seem very far away. Yet the Bible reassures us that He is near: "Though I walk through the valley of the shadow of death, I will fear no evil; for thou art with me" (Psalm 23:4). It is God's Word we should listen to, not our feelings. The state of our emotions will shift from day to day and hour to hour. But God's Word remains constant and true. God is near you, no matter what your feelings might try to tell you.

Start now

If you seriously want to win over worry, start right now by doing two things.

First, write the PRAISE + POISE + PRAYER = PEACE formula in large letters on a card and place it where you will see it every day. Attach it to the mirror where you shave or put on your makeup. Position it in a conspicuous place in your office. If you spend your time at home, place a copy over the sink or on the coffee table. If you are a driver, attach it to the sun visor in your automobile.

The more places you put the formula, the more you will be reminded of it and the more deeply it will embed itself into your consciousness.

Second, memorize Philippians 4:4-8 and repeat the words to yourself as an affirmation every morning when you wake up. In doing so, you will make these essential words of God a part of your very being. It won't take you long. And it will set you firmly on the road to success.

PART 2

HOW YOU CAN WIN

5

WIN OVER WORRY
by Rejoicing

Owen Cooper of Yazoo City, Mississippi, saw his house go up in smoke. He was one of the nation's outstanding Christian laymen and one of Mississippi's top-ranking citizens. Some members of his family barely escaped with their lives. The fire completely gutted the home and destroyed nearly everything of value.

Shortly after this terrible fire, Cooper's pastor, Dr. Harold Shirley, told me that the entire family attended a prayer meeting the following night. In that service, Owen Cooper arose during the testimony time and, with a radiance that only God can give, expressed his gratitude to the Lord for sparing their lives. He had learned years before the truth of Romans 8:28: "We know that all things work together for good to them that love God, to them who are the called according to his purpose." Despite the calamity, the inner joy of the Cooper family could not be thrown off track.

Joy is something you choose

When Paul wrote about joyfulness he did not say, "I *hope* you will be joyful." He *told* people to be joyful:

1 Thessalonians 5:16—"Rejoice evermore."

Philippians 4:4—"Rejoice in the Lord alway: and again I say, Rejoice."

Philippians 4:4 Phillips—"Delight yourselves in the Lord; yes, find your joy in him at all times."

You say, "But I don't feel like rejoicing or being happy."

By that you mean the circumstances engulfing you are not such as contribute to your joy. The majority of chronic worriers think of joyfulness as something that *happens* to them, like the sun coming out after a rainstorm. And so they make the mistake of being passive, waiting until their circumstances change.

Of course there is nothing wrong with changing difficult circumstances yourself if you have that option. But joyfulness is not a state of becoming. It is a state of being. You don't acquire joyfulness. You assume joyfulness.

Note that the apostle Paul wrote Philippians 4:4 in the imperative mood. Paul wasn't making helpful suggestions; he was giving a command. Joy is mandatory: "Rejoice in the Lord alway: and again I say, Rejoice." Literally, it could be translated, "Keep on rejoicing in the Lord always: and again I say, keep on rejoicing." Make the joy of the Lord the habitual pattern of your life. For when you fail to do this, you sin and you suffer.

The key to rejoicing is praise

You rejoice when you offer praise to God. You cannot praise God without rejoicing in God and rejoicing in the circumstances—no matter how unpleasant—that God permits.

The word "praise" in its various forms, and the word "rejoice" in its various forms, are mentioned more than 550 times in the Word of God. The very fact that this praise and rejoicing receive such frequent attention in the Bible indicates their importance.

In Psalm 34:1, David said, "I will bless the Lord at all times: his praise shall continually be in my mouth." Praise was the habit pattern of David's life, even though, like all of us, David experienced many troubles and difficulties. He often passed through deep waters. One son, Adonijah, broke his heart. Absalom, another son, betrayed him and tried to usurp his authority. Yet another son, Ammon, grieved David by committing adultery with his half-sister, Tamar. You can also read in 2 Samuel 16:5-13 how viciously Shimei cursed David, and every Sunday school pupil remembers the story of King Saul's persecution of David. Saul repeatedly sought David's life and hounded him with barbaric intensity.

Yet in all of this, David blessed the Lord and fulfilled the requirement to rejoice. God's praise was continually in David's mouth. In Psalm 33:1 David admonished, "Rejoice in the LORD, O ye righteous: for praise is comely for the upright." This was the injunction of a man who was "a man after [God's] own heart" (Acts 13:22).

After the local religious authorities in Jerusalem had mercilessly beaten Peter and the apostles for speaking "in the name of Jesus" the apostles departed, "rejoicing that they were counted worthy to suffer shame for his name" (Acts 5:40-41).

You are entitled to no particular commendation simply because you rejoice when everything goes well. When, however, you have made praise and rejoicing the pattern of your life even in difficult circumstances, you will have arrived at a place where you will not only bring glory to God, but you will also set up an immunity against worry.

Rejoice even on blue Mondays and black Fridays. Whether friends have betrayed you, neighbors are vicious and mean to you, relatives don't appreciate you, or tragedy has overtaken you, it still remains true that you can conquer worry with the attitude expressed in Isaiah 12:2,4: "Behold, God is my salvation; I will trust, and not be afraid: for the LORD JEHOVAH is my strength and my song; he also is become my salvation...And in that day shall ye say, Praise the LORD, call upon his name, declare his doings among the people, make mention that his name is exalted."

Praise is always possible

Remember what I wrote earlier: There is no condition or circumstance that can justify worry. Worry is a sin. And praise is an antidote to worry.

One of the most radiant Christian men I have ever met passed through a heart-crushing trial. To help augment the family income during the Depression, he and his wife provided room and board for a "highly respected citizen."

The man whom they took in turned out to be a Judas, a betrayer. He seduced his host's wife with diabolical cunning. When she tried to break off the relationship, he went berserk. He strangled her and then put her baby in the oven and turned on the gas, murdering the little one by asphyxiation. He then took the couple's eight-year-old son out into the garage and strangled him with a piece of wire. Finally he returned to the kitchen and lay down on some chairs in front of the stove with the gas jets wide open.

The rescue squad was able to revive the viperous murderer. But a radiant Christian man lost, in one fell swoop, his wife and children. This crushing blow would have upset the mental balance of a lesser man. Yet in the strength of the Lord this man went to the penitentiary to witness to the murderer. The way he conducted himself through that ordeal and the subsequent years has made a powerful impact on me and on thousands of others—for good and for God.

Of course this man was grief-stricken. But through it all, the joy of the Lord remained his abiding and unwavering possession.

You say you have troubles? Sure you do. We all do. But when rejoicing has become the pattern of your life, you are no longer a thermometer personality who registers the temperature of your environment. Rather, you are a thermostat personality who sets the temperature of your environment. You have learned, in the words of Paul, to "rejoice evermore" (1 Thessalonians 5:16).

Paul was no ivory-tower theorist. He urged the Christians at Philippi,

"Rejoice in the Lord alway: and again I say, Rejoice" (Philippians 4:4). At the time he wrote those words he was a prisoner in Rome. Almost certainly he knew Nero would never release him. He surely knew that ahead of him lay the executioner's sword. Yet he did not say, "Cry with me," or "Mourn with me," but "Rejoice with me."

If Paul could rejoice in such a circumstance, what excuse do we have for our anxieties?

6

WIN OVER WORRY
by Controlling Your Feelings

Norman Cousins, the famous essayist and longtime editor of the *Saturday Review*, once fell so seriously ill that doctors did not expect him to live.

Cousins took stock. He concluded that if bad emotions can induce illness, good emotions should do the reverse. He determined to think and act in a cheerful, positive, and upbeat manner on the premise that "a merry heart doeth good like a medicine" (Proverbs 17:22). It worked. And Cousins survived to write a book about the experience, titled *Anatomy of an Illness*.

Take hold of your emotional steering wheel

It is a basic law of human nature that you will feel as you think and act. Think and act the way you want to feel, and soon you will feel the way you are thinking and acting. Ideally this will be the way God wants you to feel. Let me give you an illustration.

Go to a quiet room, stand with your feet about a foot apart at the heels, and clasp your hands behind your back, letting them hang loosely. Bow your back and neck and head slightly, maintaining complete relaxation of the body. Now start thinking resentful thoughts.

Did you observe what happened? Immediately you straightened up because of the contraction of your muscles. You became taut. Your thoughts, feelings, and actions interrelated.

When a man comes into my study and sits down in a relaxed manner and leans back, I know he has absolute confidence in me. He has no fear of me, for a position of defense would be hard to assume from this posture.

Carry this over into your everyday life. When you are depressed and forlorn and feel that you have nothing but trouble, then smile. Throw your shoulders back. Take a good deep breath. Sing. Better still, force yourself to laugh. Keep forcing it until you are laughing heartily. At first it will seem mockery, but I guarantee you, it will chase away your gloom.

You cannot think fearfully and act courageously at the same time. Conversely, you cannot think courageously and act fearfully. You cannot think hatred and act kindly at the same time. Conversely, you cannot think kindly and act hatefully. Your feelings inevitably correspond to your dominant thoughts and actions. Is this scriptural? Absolutely! God's Word says, "For as he thinketh in his heart, so is he" (Proverbs 23:7).

Alfred Adler, the famous Austrian psychiatrist who served as visiting professor at Columbia University in New York and at the Long Island School of Medicine, taught that those who are immersed in helping others do not suffer neuroses, psychoses, or feelings of inferiority. Indeed, financial generosity and its corollary, compassion in positive action, strengthens and even sustains the kind of poise that is otherwise impossible.

How thought and body are linked

Now once again, read Philippians 4:8:

> Finally, brethren, whatsoever things are true, whatsoever things are honest, whatsoever things are just, whatsoever things are pure, whatsoever things are lovely, whatsoever things are of

good report; if there be any virtue, and if there be any praise, think on these things (Philippians 4:8).

Obedience to the command of Philippians 4:8 will result in obedience to the command of Philippians 4:4. As you think, so will you feel. Our feelings are revealed by our actions.

For instance, when I see a man with his feet set at ten minutes to two and his lips at twenty past eight, who pushes his weight instead of carrying it, I say to myself, "Watch out. This man is a potential tyrant." When I see a woman nervously moving her wedding band back and forth on her ring finger, I surmise that she and her husband are not getting along too well. I'm usually right.

No, you might not be able to directly control your feelings. But you *can* control your thoughts and actions. Therefore, in the strength of Christ, master your thoughts and actions, and thus dominate your feelings. It is impossible for you to "rejoice in the Lord alway" and to worry at the same time. Furthermore, you cannot remove thoughts of worry and fear simply by saying, "I don't want to be afraid. I don't want to worry."

To win over worry, discipline yourself to think upon "these things" of Philippians 4:8. Let your actions accommodate themselves to your thoughts. Discipline yourself to smile, to maintain good posture, to talk with a musical voice in a dynamic manner—in short, to act in a manner compatible with these positive thoughts.

Don't start tomorrow; start today. Start now. Your worries will flee, and God will be glorified.

Controlling thoughts and actions neutralize the divided mind

Bob Glaze of Dallas, Texas, distinguished himself as a Bible teacher, a patron of the arts, a civic leader, a family man, and a businessman. He sat on the president's council of the Dallas Symphony Association. He taught a Bible class every Sunday morning for more than 40 years and was written up in such prestigious business publications as *Fortune* as an outstanding businessman.

Bob was a certified public accountant by profession. Things went very well for him from the time he was discharged from the navy, where he served as an officer during World War II. After several years as a comptroller for a large organization, he and three friends decided to go into business for themselves. The business collapsed within a year. Bob did not panic or go into the trough of depression. He took control of his situation and, like a superb sea captain, skillfully maneuvered the ship of his life through dangerous and uncharted waters.

Bob would not compromise and accept just any job that came along. He determined what he would like to do and with whom he would like to be associated. His number one choice was America's leading developer, Trammell Crow of Dallas.

Bob had heard that Trammell Crow was a fitness buff. So Bob got into first-class shape himself. He was 43 years old at the time. He set an appointment to meet with Trammell Crow. During the interview, Trammell suggested they visit the fourteenth floor of one of his buildings.

Bob had heard that Trammell did not take elevators, but rather, ran up stairways. When Trammell arrived at the fourteenth floor, Bob was right behind him. Later Bob chuckled as he recounted the experience and said, "I don't know if Trammell hired me because he thought I was a good man for the job or because he was impressed that I could stay with him up the fourteen flights of stairs!"

The point I'm making is that Bob kept his focus so tightly on his objective that he did not permit a divided mind. He gave no room to worry at all. He controlled his feelings by controlling his thoughts and his actions. And he secured the position he wanted, to the delight of both Trammell Crow and himself.

Controlling thoughts and actions restores health

In November 1986, Bob was rushed to the hospital with a severe case of pancreatitis. His sickness and the complications from it lasted for more than seven months. The cause of the problem lay in his gall bladder. However, Bob was so weak that his doctors could not take the chance of operating on him. For weeks on end, he was fed intravenously. Three times, according to the doctors, they nearly lost him.

After his gall bladder surgery, Bob announced to the doctors the day he would go home. They were skeptical, but Bob acted on the conviction that the surgery was a success and that he would return home earlier than the doctors had originally suggested. And he did.

Bob wasn't imprudent; he was simply positive. In later life, he worked at a pace that would challenge many a younger man. He acknowledged that God supernaturally intervened in restoring him to health. He and his wife, Ruth, believed that God heard the prayers of literally thousands of Christian friends around the world while he was in the hospital. And he was quick to give God the glory, as are all of us who had a share in helping to love him and pray him through this ordeal.

But note that during this time, Bob never permitted himself to focus his attention on anything except the expectation that he would survive, get well, and live a vigorous and fruitful life. I submit to you that God honored Bob's faith and the faith of his friends. And God also honored the focus of his mind, which gave foundation to the kinds of emotions that are helpful in healing.

Take control of your thoughts and feelings, and, I am certain, God will honor your faith too.

Kick the habit of defeatism

Much damage is done to the cause of Christ by professing Christians who shout out their defeatism and negativism by the limp manner in which they shake hands, the listless way in which they walk, the sourpuss countenance they maintain, and the plaintive and whining way in which they speak. I believe these people do more damage to the cause of Christ than all of the bootleggers, extortionists, whoremongers, drunkards, and gutter riffraff put together.

When I was pastor of a large church in a Southern city, I faced problems that would have challenged my sanity had it not been for the grace of God. One particular problem came to my attention and the attention of several other church officers. A senior deacon was enmeshed in sin. He showed no signs of remorse nor any desire to repent. Evidence also emerged that another prominent member of the church was stealing more than $160 a week from the Sunday school offerings. We faced a tough dilemma. If we made either matter public, it could cause irreparable damage to the testimony of Christ.

In addition to these problems, my wife and I had sorrow in our home. Our precious little son was totally paralyzed. He suffered from cerebral palsy as a result of birth injuries caused by an intoxicated doctor. The little fellow hovered between life and death.

Given all these pressures, I could easily have caved in to worry. But I settled my mind on Psalm 1. As never before I learned to appreciate the wisdom of that blessed man who delights in the law of the Lord day and night (verses 1-2). I did not want to feel as I was feeling. It was not a good testimony. Therefore, by God's grace, I fastened my thoughts upon the "these things" of Philippians 4:8 and endeavored to act in a compatible manner.

On several occasions I got into my car, drove outside the city, and literally forced myself to laugh and to sing. I'm sure some passersby thought I was crazy. But this was what helped keep me sane!

Think and act the way God would have you to think and act. Result? You will feel as you think and act. This, in turn, will glorify God. And it will help you give worry the brush-off.

From bicycles to banking

Dr. Mochtar Riady, an ethnic Chinese Indonesian, always had his heart set on banking. Fifty years ago, it was not possible for ethnic Chinese to work in prestigious positions. Yet Riady never lost his focus nor weakened in his determination to someday go into the banking business.

While he was waiting, he began importing and selling spare parts for bicycles. The day came when he was given a menial job at a bank.

He worked fervently and faithfully. During this time he pursued his studies. He kept up an incredible pace until he earned a doctorate.

He formed the now world-famous Lippo Group of companies, including Lippo Bank and later the Lippo Life Insurance Company. He developed a multinational business that included banking, insurance, urban development, retailing, properties, healthcare, education, and the Internet.

In a period of less than three years, Dr. Riady and son, James, developed a 600-acre nondescript piece of land into a "city of tomorrow." Many global business analysts considered Lippo Karawaci the most advanced community in Asia; some consider it the most advanced in the world.

Dr. Riady also made arrangements for his sons to receive the best possible academic education, as well as practical education (working in financial, insurance, and property institutions). On many occasions he laid everything on the line and exposed himself to what could have been financial disaster. Through it all, he treated people fairly and ensured that they would enjoy value-added benefits by their alliance with his businesses.

When Dr. Riady bought the 600 acres, he saw to it that all the people in the area were provided better homes than they had previously known, as well as employment opportunities previously denied to them. He built a 300-bed hospital, a five-star hotel, and housing that compared favorably with the upscale residential districts of any city on earth. And his sons developed great business capabilities and demonstrated unusual acumen coupled with superior human relations skills.

On many occasions, Dr. Riady suffered opposition ranging from severe invectives to cruel betrayals. However, he never lost his upbeat, optimistic mind-set. He controlled his feelings and thus controlled his environment. He did not allow his environment to control him.

During a time of financial troubles in southeast Asia, some Indonesians, angered by what they perceived to be political corruption, unleashed their hostility on Dr. Riady. The damage to Lippo Kara-waci amounted to millions of dollars. Yet I never heard of complaints from Dr. Riady. He must have suffered profound grief when some of those whom he had emancipated from poverty took part in vandaliz-ing and looting the stores and factories in Lippo Karawaci.

During the 1990s, the Riadys were scandalized by politicians and pundits who accused them of guilt by association. It is a long story. The Riadys did not defend themselves; they simply put their confidence in God and waited patiently for the truth to finally emerge.

When one walks into Dr. Riady's office, the most striking aspect of the office décor is a magnificent artistic portrayal of Jesus wash-ing the disciples' feet. During a visit in 1997, I was struck by the quiet presence of Mrs. Riady in the corner of the office preparing her Bible study lesson.

Dr. Riady, a convert to the Lord Jesus Christ in his mature years and after verifiable success in business, demonstrates day by day the power of controlling one's feelings. He carries an emotional thermo-stat that sets the temperature around him—not a thermometer that merely responds to his environment.

7

WIN OVER WORRY
by Counting Your Many Blessings

There is a story of a king who was so unhappy that he dispatched one of his men to go find a happy man. The king ordered, "When you find the happy man, purchase his shirt and bring it back to me that I might wear it and also be happy."

For years the king's emissary traveled and searched. He could not find a happy man. Finally, one day when he was walking in one of the poorer quarters of one of the poorest countries, he heard a man singing at the top of his voice. He followed the sound and found a man who was plowing a field.

He asked the plowman, "Are you happy?"

The plowman replied, "I have never known a day of unhappiness."

The king's representative then told the plowman the purpose of his mission. The plowman laughed uproariously as he replied, "Why, I don't have a shirt!"

Get out your calculator

To utilize the tonic of praise as an antidote to worry, you must develop a healthy respect and gratitude for the good things God has already given you. When you're feeling down, you may have to "gird up the loins of your mind" and make a determined effort to focus your attention. God has lavishly bestowed blessings on you; don't take them for granted.

Your blessings may not be material blessings, but they are real blessings nevertheless. Actually, no man has ever found joy simply because he acquired material gain. Joy does not consist in the abundance of our material possessions; "a man's life consisteth not in the abundance of the things which he possesseth" (Luke 12:15).

Some time ago I entertained, as my luncheon guest, Jean Baptiste Mugarura from Rwanda. This six-foot, two-inch, 35-year-old African took the Haggai Institute Advanced Leadership Training program in Singapore in 1999. He was one of the youngest ever to be invited to the program.

Until five years ago, he served as an official in the National Bank of Rwanda (much like the Federal Reserve Bank of the United States). Then came the massacres inflicted upon the Rwandan people by rebel forces. Among those murdered by the rebels were John's fiancée and his mentor. Also, two of the mentor's three children were killed. John's mentor, arguably one of the two most influential people in Rwanda, had exerted every effort to bring peace. Yet the rebels slaughtered him. More than one million in this country were killed.

John entered the dark night of the soul. These were days of deep reflection and self-examination. Yet if you could sit across the table from this radiant executive, now serving the Lord in Rwanda and influencing people across the world, you would never guess he had endured such an experience.

How do I account for it? This man understands the peace formula: PRAISE + POISE + PRAYER = PEACE.

In the meantime, the Lord has given him a beautiful wife. He is now thoroughly immersed in full-time Christian work. He carries the workload of two active leaders. And he is bringing hope and help to the devastated families of Rwanda. Without his ingrained and

Spirit-motivated habit of counting his blessings, he could have shriveled up and become bitter and useless.

So, consider your blessings.

For how much money would you sell the health that God has given to you? How much does your wife's love mean to you? Have you ever thoroughly appreciated your child's devotion? For what amount would you sell your reputation if it could be put on the open market? What premium do you put upon the eyesight God has given you? What about the capacity to hear, and to speak, and to feel, and to taste? Have you ever thought about how impoverished you would be if suddenly you were deprived of all your friends?

We tend to take the manifold blessings of God for granted, don't we? Start counting your blessings; your heart will overflow with gratitude and your lips with praise.

As one well-known quatrain reminds us:

> I had the blues
> Because I had no shoes;
> Until upon the street
> I met a man who had no feet.

Count your blessings. If it will help you, take time every now and then to write out your blessings on a piece of paper. Praise God for the love of your wife, the affection of your children, your good health, the encouragement of your friends.

As you exert some effort along this line, blessings by the score will come crowding into your consciousness. You will soon feel your heart singing, "Praise God from whom all blessings flow!" And you will be honoring the Lord as you obey the exhortation in Philippians 4:4 that we are to rejoice always.

Read what the Bible says about God's blessings:

> How precious also are thy thoughts unto me, O God! How
> great is the sum of them! If I should count them, they are

more in number than the sand: when I awake, I am still with thee (Psalm 139:17-18).

Many, O LORD my God, are thy wonderful works which thou hast done, and thy thoughts which are to usward: they cannot be reckoned up in order unto thee: if I would declare and speak of them, they are more than can be numbered (Psalm 40:5).

Keep praising through disaster

Spurgeon, the great Baptist preacher of the nineteenth century, wrote of a young man who had suffered an accident in which he had broken his hip. The hip did not heal properly, which left the man crippled. People prayed earnestly that God would restore this young man to health and strength. Shortly after they began their intense and concerted intercession on behalf of this young man, apparent tragedy struck. The young man fell and broke his hip again.

What were they to make of this? It would have been completely natural for them to abandon their intercession, for the man's condition had clearly worsened, not improved. Fortunately, however, many of the intercessors—wise and mature Christians—saw God's hand in the entire affair.

They continued praising God and thanking Him. As it turned out, because the hip had been "broken" a second time, it had now set perfectly. It wasn't long until convalescence under God's leadership had done its perfect work. The young man walked with no limp whatsoever. The second tragedy ended up being a blessing in disguise.

Count your blessings! Even when things seem to go wrong, thank God and take courage. Say with the apostle Paul, "Most gladly therefore will I rather glory in my infirmities, that the power of Christ may rest upon me" (2 Corinthians 12:9).

In the previous chapter I mentioned my son Johnny. In 1950, the Lord blessed us with this precious baby boy. After the disastrous circumstances of his birth, the little fellow nearly died. Though God was pleased to spare him, he was now totally paralyzed. He had a keen mind and all the inclinations and desires of a normal boy, but his body would not respond to the demands of his will. That hurt him and us. However, God gave him a marvelously sweet disposition.

Was our son's paralysis a blessing? Yes, definitely so. Between the year of his birth and the year I resigned the pastorate to go into full-time evangelism, I buried more infants and ministered to more sick children than any other pastor I'm aware of. God had conditioned me in a special way for this unusual and blessed ministry.

The life of my son was a deep blessing within our family. There are many ways in which I could demonstrate this, but they involve experiences locked up in the cherished and secret places of my heart, and are open only to God and our immediate family.

Johnny died in 1975, 16 years after the first edition of *How to Win Over Worry* was published. People came from as far as 5,000 miles away to attend his funeral. One man who drove from a distant city said, "I never knew exactly how to express to Johnny what an inspiration he was to me. I wanted to come here because I'm sure he's conscious of this service, and I just want him to know how much he meant to me."

Have the blessings given to us through Johnny survived the test of time? Indeed they have. Despite my thumbprint eyebrows, my foghorn voice, and my stern looks, children seem to gravitate to me. I believe I carry on a more profound correspondence with children than anyone outside the fields of teaching or child psychology. I can walk into a room in which a baby is crying, speak a few words, and the baby will stop crying. That I consider to be a blessing, and I must count it.

I must also count it a blessing that Christine and I have survived six decades of marriage. The reason I say "survive" is that invalidism in the home does not bring you together; it drives you apart.

Elizabeth B. Brown, the wife of the celebrated medical doctor Paul Brown of Tennessee, wrote of their having a sick child in the home for five years. She marveled that the two of them were able to manage it and survive the stress. According to William G. Justice, who in 1982 wrote *When Death Comes*, "Ninety percent of all couples who have lost a child to death have serious marital problems within months of the death of their child. Three out of four divorce within two years."

Praise works in the toughest places

In a West Asian nation, a young minister of the gospel preaches to between 1,200 and 1,500 people every Sunday. In that same nation, people have been slaughtered by the thousands. When I met with this remarkable minister in a neutral capital of the world, I said, "How do you handle the pressure of trying to maintain a ministry in a city and nation vocally committed to the destruction of Christianity?"

He smiled at me and said, "How good is God—what blessings He bestows!"

I thought to myself, *This poor fellow didn't hear what I said.* But then the minister went on to explain.

"God has put us in the eye of the storm. On one side are the Marxists. On the other side are extremist Muslims. They are in such hostile combat with each other that by being in the center we are wonderfully protected. Better still, hundreds are coming to know Christ as Savior." This man was not bemoaning his lot; he was counting his blessings. I don't think that worry finds him a suitable host.

During my visits to Vietnam in the late 1960s and early 1970s, I met with many Vietnamese people. One man stood out. He told me how he regretted the war and how sorry he was that it was necessary for American soldiers to come and suffer separation from home, physical injury, and even death. Then he said, "The greatest victory of this conflict is that the Americans and the Koreans brought the gospel to our village, and we who were in darkness came to know Jesus Christ."

This man had lost members of his family. He had lost his business, and his home had been burned to the ground. Even then, he knew how to count his blessings!

During the Korean conflict of 1950–53, Presbyterian missionary

Dr. Harold Voelkel had a penetrating and pervasive ministry among the troops on both sides. He personally won to faith in Christ more than 150 North Korean soldiers, 20 of whom are now in full-time gospel ministry.

It was Voelkel who introduced my mother and father, so I have more than a casual appreciation for that gentleman. The character quality that captured my attention, every time I met him, was his buoyant and resilient Christian optimism in any situation. He knew how to count his blessings, and worry never seemed to catch up with him.

Count your blessings, name them one by one; and it will surprise you what the Lord has done. And one of the greatest surprises will be the fact that you are no longer saddled by that monster, worry, who has been riding hard on you.

Let me urge again that when you become depressed and worried you should take a piece of paper and literally force yourself to write out every blessing that comes to mind. Concentrate. Think hard. Sure, it will take time, but not as much time as worrying will. It won't take as much time as an interview at a psychiatrist's office, and it will be considerably cheaper. Furthermore, in the strength of God you will be actively doing something about your own condition. Counting your blessings is much more effective than passively submitting to psychotherapy.

I'm not saying that psychotherapy has no place, or that severe psychiatric conditions do not need a specialist's attention. Psychiatrists and counselors can provide enormous help in the right situations.

But, there are many people who frequent the offices of psychiatrists and counselors who could be enjoying full mental and emotional health right now had they only taken certain precautions and observed the biblical formula that can free them from worry: PRAISE + POISE + PRAYER = PEACE.

It's a formula that works.

8

WIN OVER WORRY
by Mastering the Art of Altruism

A young college man sought counseling from Dr. George W. Truett, who, at the time, was the pastor of First Baptist Church of Dallas, Texas. The student had passed through troubled waters. He said he was ready to give up his faith and that he had lost all confidence in God and people.

Dr. Truett listened to this young man. When the student finished his tale of woe, the wise and patient pastor asked the young man for a favor. The young man agreed. Dr. Truett then gave the young man the name of a hospital and the room number of a patient who was in need of a visit. Said the greathearted minister, "I just don't have time to make the visit. You make it for me." The young man assented.

As a favor to the mighty pastor in Dallas, the young man determined to do his best. He did so well that he became genuinely interested in the patient. In so doing, his own difficulties and despair were dispelled. He came away from that hospital a new man.

In 1981, I returned to the lovely island of Bali in Indonesia. Because rooms were difficult to obtain, I did not stay at my usual stopping place, the Bali Intercontinental, but instead secured accommodations at the Bali Hyatt. When I arrived and started up the steps to the entrance, several of the hotel personnel said, "Welcome to the Bali Hyatt, Dr. Haggai. Michael, our general manager, has reserved for you the best suite in the hotel. You are his guest, and you won't pay for anything."

I expressed amazement. When I attempted to check in at the registration desk, one of the general manager's assistants said, "Oh, no, that is already taken care of. Let me escort you to your room." He took me to one of the most elegant suites I have ever seen in all my world travels.

Within minutes, the general manager, Michael, came to my suite. I tried to express my thanks.

"You don't remember me, do you?" he said.

"No, and I apologize," I said.

He said, "In the 1960s when you stayed at the Singapore Intercontinental, I was a bellman, hustling bags. Every time you came, you treated me just as grandly as you treated your friend, the general manager, George Milne. From that time onward I harbored a secret dream that someday I would be in charge of my own hotel and be able to show you my gratitude for the encouragement and inspiration you gave me."

Later that same year at Brisbane Airport, when I was ready to board a plane headed for Sydney, I heard an announcement over the loudspeaker that the flight had been cancelled due to bad weather conditions. The passengers vented their anger on that poor Ansett Airways agent in a way I've rarely heard before. I watched the way he handled them. When things quieted down and most of them had left, I walked up to him and said, "Congratulations on the masterful way you handled a situation over which you had no control. You will be the winner, believe me." He thanked me warmly, and I went back to the hotel.

A year and a half later, I was at the same airport with a coach ticket for Sydney. One of the lady agents came up to me and said, "Aren't you Dr. Haggai?"

"Yes, I am."

"Would you come this way, please?"

I followed her and was astonished when she said, "I need your ticket. We are replacing it with a first-class ticket, our compliments." When she saw my surprise, she explained, "Our manager said that last year, when people were so angry that at one point he wondered if they were going to do him bodily harm, you were the one person that kept cool and even encouraged him. This is his way—and our way—of thanking you."

I share these stories with you to demonstrate how you can conquer worry by mastering the art of altruism. Become genuinely interested in other people. Love your neighbor as yourself. Honor God by losing your life in serving others. By others I am referring not only to your employer or your family, but also to people you don't know whom God gives you the privilege of serving.

Take the initiative

Uncle Joe Hawk was one of the most radiant personalities I have ever met. For more than half a century he was a member of the First Baptist Church of Cleveland, Tennessee. When I met him he was 87 years old, but younger than many 25-year-olds. He attended every service I conducted in that good church in 1953. Let me share with you a little about his sparkling vitality as an octogenarian.

Years before, during the Great Depression, the church was in straitened circumstances. Uncle Joe Hawk was a drayman (one who hauls goods). He had been blessed with a good business, but of course he was suffering just like other businessmen during those hard years. Nevertheless, this dear man continued to put first his concern for that church and its people, many of whom had not yet accepted Christ.

At considerable personal risk, Uncle Joe sold his two finest dray horses. He gave the money to the church. Because of his gift, the First Baptist Church of Cleveland, Tennessee, stands as a mighty citadel for Christ today. Few people knew about what he had done. He had done it without fanfare. In fact, many of the church members today are unaware of his tremendous sacrifice.

Uncle Joe never got the money back from the church. He didn't expect to, and he didn't want it. He gave it for the sheer joy of giving. He gave it to the eternal glory of God and for the spiritual profit of man. No man who is that interested in others has time to worry about his own problems.

When was the last time you sacrificed and sent anonymously a gift of $50 over and above your tithe to a college or seminary student who was having a hard time? When was the last time you gave something to someone anonymously—a gesture that could in no way profit you from a material standpoint?

You may say you have no money. But you don't need vast reserves of cash to be generous to others. For example:

- Perhaps the mother next door is sick and in great need of help. Why not offer to take care of the children for a couple of days? True, they may be little monsters. But that is what makes your help so valuable to their mother.

- When your neighbor goes on vacation, why not offer to take care of the mail and send it on?

- Why not drop a line of appreciation to that teacher who has taken such an interest in your child and made such a distinct contribution to his or her highest good?

- Drop a line of gratitude to your pastor for the message that was such a blessing to you. Encourage him. It will take only a few moments. If you send your note by e-mail, doing this won't even cost you a stamp.

Does not the Word of God tell us we are to esteem others better than ourselves? "Let nothing be done through strife or vainglory; but in lowliness of mind let each esteem other better than themselves" (Philippians 2:3).

Let me earnestly suggest that you determine to do something specific for someone every day—something for which no remuneration of any kind will be sought or expected. What use is morality if it isn't proactive? And besides, doing this will relieve you of the time you normally give to worrying. Your cup will run over with the joy of the Lord.

Go ahead; do it now. If it doesn't come to you easily and if you don't know how to begin, simply sit down and ask the Lord to guide you. With pencil and paper in hand, write down some ideas that come to your mind.

Perhaps the Lord will lead you to do the washing for the lady next door who has been hampered by her day-and-night care of sick children. Perhaps you will contact the head of some fine Christian college or seminary to secure the name of a student who is in great need. Or you may be led to invite a lonely church member to have dinner with you on Sunday. With just a little thought, you will be able to come up with many more ideas. Just go do it!

Putting yourself out for others is like a healthy diet

I am persuaded that my mother, who suffered major illnesses for the last 45 years of her life, lived to such a great age and with such great satisfaction because she immersed herself in serving others.

When a family moved into the neighborhood, she would take some warm food to them while they were getting settled. When someone was sick, she would take a card to them, as well as a thoughtful little present. She maintained correspondence with hundreds of people around the world.

I believe that serving others created in my mother a greater capacity to praise God. She was a mild-mannered lady, quiet of demeanor, but a person of strong will and great capacity to care for others. To this day, nearly a decade after her final illness and death, people all over the world still talk to me about her. They will tell me of some little act of kindness that she had shown toward them. They will produce a postcard, a letter, or a greeting card that she had mailed to them.

One of my mother's close friends died in 1939 in Massachusetts. Mother maintained contact with the four daughters, their spouses, and the grandchildren from 1945, when she left Massachusetts, until late 1978, when she became bedridden.

It is giving, not getting, that induces praise. It is serving, not being served, that develops the highest type of rejoicing. And, of course, no one can rejoice and worry at the same time. The two are mutually exclusive.

If you want to find real joy in living and a genuine escape from worrying, get involved in helping others. That will leave you no time to worry.

Life offers countless opportunities for altruism

A friend of mine, Elmer G. Leterman, visited Honolulu in 1935.

In those days, the main mode of travel from the East Coast of the United States to Hawaii was by ship. When Elmer and his wife arrived, they descended the gangplank and were greeted effusively by friends who put leis around their necks. He noticed there were hundreds of people disembarking whom had no one waiting to greet them or give them leis.

Elmer had hardly unpacked his suitcase at the hotel before he determined that as long as he was in Hawaii, he would meet every boat with a sufficient number of leis to welcome every person who did not have someone waiting to meet him and put a lei around his neck with the robust "aloha" and hospitality for which Hawaii is internationally known.

As it turned out, the people whom he greeted in this way gave him multiplied millions of dollars of business over the next 40 years, even though that was the last thing on his mind. Elmer was a happy man, always upbeat. He had mastered the art of altruism. And it left no room for a divided mind.

The late Ee Peng Liang of Singapore had earned the respect not only of the people in Singapore, but of people around the world who had watched his humanitarian efforts over the years. He was a chartered accountant by profession and headed up a substantial business in Singapore.

The man never ceased to amaze me in his capacity for remembering detail. I met him once. Afterward, I would periodically get a note from him with a warm greeting. There was absolutely nothing I could do for him in a business or personal sense except assure him of my continued friendship and respect. But Ee Peng Liang did not do what he did in order to get things from others. He had mastered the art of altruism and impressed me as being one of the most worry-free men I have met in the course of my travels.

Help those who need help in ways they really need it

By all means, use common sense in your efforts to assist other people. Don't be like a certain young Cub Scout who had his own ideas on the subject. One night during a pack meeting the scoutmaster asked all those who had done their good deed for the day to lift their hands. All hands were lifted except the hand of this one scout.

The scoutmaster barked out, "Jimmy, go out and do your good deed for the day and don't come back until you have done it."

Jimmy was gone for about 20 minutes. When he returned, his clothes were in shreds, his hair was disheveled, and his face was cut and bleeding.

The scoutmaster said, "Jimmy, what have you been doing?"

The boy replied, "I did my good deed for the day, sir."

"What was that?" asked the scoutmaster.

"I helped an old lady across the street, sir."

"Well," said the scoutmaster, "how on earth did you get in that condition?"

"She didn't want to go," replied Jimmy.

Use common sense in your effort to help others. For example, during the darkest part of the Great Depression, a needy family was given an expensive, pedigreed French poodle. Doubtless there is much good to be said about a French poodle. But the friend who gave the dog would have been much wiser and more helpful if she had taken the same money and purchased needed clothing and food for the family.

Assist other people at their point of greatest need. And while doing so, remember that "it is more blessed to give than to receive" (Acts 20:35).

Kindness kills worry every time

Your genuine interest in other people will assassinate the monster of worry. Your positive thoughts of concern for others will crowd out negative, fear-producing anxiety.

Reflect once again upon the concern our Lord showed for others. Even while dying, He showed compassion to His enemies and cried out, "Father, forgive them; for they know not what they do" (Luke 23:34). And while He was in great agony upon the cross, He showed concern for His mother and made the finest possible preparations for her after His departure.

Real Christian discipline in the strength of God is required to master the art of altruism, but the rewards are immeasurable—especially as they relate to the altruist. Without exception, the people who are always rejoicing are people who have mastered this art of altruism, of being genuinely interested in others. This rejoicing chases away gloom and kills worry.

You will rejoice in the Lord always as you faithfully fulfill the injunction in Galatians 6:2-4: "Bear ye one another's burdens, and so fulfill the law of Christ. For if a man think himself to be something, when he is nothing, he deceiveth himself. But let every man prove his own work, and then shall he have rejoicing in himself alone, and not in another."

I share with you these same verses from the Amplified Bible:

> Bear (endure, carry) one another's burdens and troublesome moral faults, and in this way fulfill and observe perfectly the law of Christ (the Messiah) and complete what is lacking [in your obedience to it]. For if any person thinks himself to be somebody [too important to condescend to shoulder

another's load] when he is nobody [of superiority except in his own estimation], he deceives and deludes and cheats himself. But let every person carefully scrutinize and examine and test his own conduct and his own work. He can then have the personal satisfaction and joy of doing something commendable [in itself alone] without [resorting to] boastful comparison with his neighbor (Galatians 6:2-4).

9

WIN OVER WORRY
by Never Expecting Thanks

Illustrating a sermon, Dr. R.A. Torrey once told a story he had heard about a shipwreck in Lake Michigan. A powerful swimmer, he recalled, who was then a student at Northwestern University, had rescued 23 people as the ship went down.

To Dr. Torrey's astonishment, an elderly man at the back of the hall raised his hand. "I was that man," he said.

Dr. Torrey asked him what stood out most in his memory about that experience after all the intervening years.

The rescuer lowered his eyes, and in a quiet voice replied, "Not a one said thanks."

Don't expect to be appreciated. When you are appreciated, it will be like the cherry on top of the whipped cream of your strawberry sundae—something a little special. But don't let your rejoicing be dependent upon appreciation shown to you.

Our Lord healed ten lepers. Do you remember how many came back to thank Him? That's right—one!

The late General Harry C. Trexler, a wealthy philanthropist and outstanding citizen of Allentown, Pennsylvania, provided for the financial needs of 40 college students in 1933—the year in which he died.

Four months before his death he called upon his secretary and inquired how many young men and women he was sending through college. She told him. With a mixture of bewilderment and grief he replied, "And last Christmas I got only one or two Christmas cards from this group."

Some time ago, I read about a man in New York who, over a period of more than four decades, helped more than 5,000 young people secure jobs in New York City. Recalling it later, he observed that only six had expressed gratitude.

The lesson? Expect ingratitude. Be generous for the joy of generosity, but don't expect to receive thanks. Give for the joy of giving, and soon you will be so thrillingly occupied with the privilege of giving that you will not have time to reflect upon the ingratitude of the recipients.

Ingratitude is the human condition

It is quite evident as you read the Pauline epistles that some of the very people whom Paul won to faith in Jesus Christ turned upon him and reviled him maliciously. Paul reveals to us in Romans 1:21 that ingratitude is at the root of all sin—whether that ingratitude be active or passive: "When they knew God, they glorified him not as God, neither were thankful; but became vain in their imaginations, and their foolish heart was darkened."

Was not ingratitude the root of the sin committed by Adam and Eve?

Consider it. The Lord Jesus Christ died for us "while we were yet sinners" (Romans 5:8). He suffered. He bled. He died—for us. Yet there are millions who, knowing this, refuse to accept Him as Savior and Lord. Why? Ingratitude!

Have you ever read about Aristotle's ideal man? Here is the philosopher's definition of him: "The ideal man takes joy in doing favors for others; but he feels ashamed to have others do favors for him. For it is a mark of superiority to confer a kindness; but it is a mark of inferiority to receive it."

Acts 20:35 says "it is more blessed to give than to receive." Therefore, let your joy arise out of the blessedness of giving, of helping, of doing. Don't expect gratitude; find your joy in the very act of service. Years ago, Samuel Johnson said, "Gratitude is a fruit of great cultivation; you do not find it among gross people."

People just don't make the effort

Remember those times when your friends moved away to distant locations? No doubt you waxed eloquent and emotional about how you'd stay in touch, write, phone, e-mail, and visit. Think back and ask yourself how often such resolutions were actually carried out—whether it was with your gang at the college dorm, your buddies in the military service, your neighbors down the street, the friends you met on a six-day cruise overseas, your coworkers at the office or factory, or whatever.

It's not that we intend to ignore our friends. It's the apathy within us that does the work. Unless you take measures to counteract that apathy, you'll lose the benefit of continuing relationships and uplifting experiences. And when you examine your heart, you'll not find it so difficult to grasp why others are also apathetic.

Take the matter of class reunions. Usually there are one or two spark plugs in the class who bring it all together. Were it not for them, no reunions would happen. They are the ones who take action, aggressively contact all the other members, and take steps to bring about a thoroughly delightful experience of getting together after years of absence from each other.

You may have heard the saying, "He who would have friends must show himself friendly." And maintaining friendships takes discipline, time, and energy. To the degree that you understand the natural inclination toward apathy in your own life and grasp the insight regarding those whom you feel should not be apathetic to you, to that degree you will increase your capacity for the component of praise, the deterrent to worry and its divided mind.

I have talked many times about ingratitude to my esteemed long-time colleague Dr. William M. "Bill" Hinson, who earned his doctorate in behavioral modification. We have noted how, when you go out of your way to assist somebody, that person sometimes seems to resent you. It's almost as if he or she is saying, "I could have made it on my own. I do not need you." This used to sting me.

I remember sitting in a restaurant in a Florida city one morning when a young minister in his early thirties wept unashamedly in frustration over the church he was pastoring. He said, "For the Lord's sake, get me out of here." Then he suggested a church he would like to pastor.

Another great friend, E. Harold Keown, Sr., and I immediately went into action. We knew that the Lord would have to open the door, but we were going to do everything possible to remove any obstructions. After a significant expenditure of our time and even money, the church called the young man. Since then, he has never said, "Thank you." He has never acknowledged that we did anything to help him. In fact, he has snubbed both of us. He is a good man, an outstanding speaker, and he has developed into a superior leader. Gratitude, however, does not seem to be high on his scale of personality characteristics.

When you help others, anticipate apathy. A young dentist in our city phoned me out of desperation one night to tell me his wife was on the threshold of suicide. I immediately made time to see this very attractive and capable young couple. We prayed together. The Lord spared her. Shortly thereafter, not only did he never say thank you, he also became critical of the very work in which I am involved.

King Saul never showed a genuine gratitude to David even though David saved his life and kingdom. Saul, who was jealous of David, tried to kill him on more than one occasion. Don't be surprised if you are not appreciated.

I know many parents—friends of mine—who have immersed their children in material benefits, only to find that the children don't seem to appreciate it. The parents often ask me why.

I have said to fathers who started with nothing and struggled to get where they are, "Where would you be today if your father had done for you what you have done for your children?" In each case, they either blanched or said something like, "Whew, I never thought of that." I am convinced that drowning children with material blessings risks producing ingratitude that will plague them throughout life.

The famous international investor Sir John Templeton warned that in giving great wealth to our children we run the risk of breeding pride in them. They did not earn their money. Consequently, they will always wonder if they could have made it without the largesse handed to them.

One young man said to me, "I'm a self-made man." I replied, "If you didn't share your father's name, do you think the bank would have approved the loans you have taken out? They loaned you millions of dollars without sufficient collateral simply because you are your father's son!"

Ingratitude is a universal sin. Expect it. Give for the joy of giving. Do for the joy of doing. Help only for the joy of helping. And you won't have time even to notice the prevalence of the sin of ingratitude. Lifting praise up to God should be the pattern of your life—regardless of the cold and even cruel treatment you might receive from some whom you have helped.

10

WIN OVER WORRY
by Thought Control

In the first church I served as pastor, there was a young lady 29 years of age who wore a facial expression that reminded me of an approaching cyclone.

It came as no surprise to me to discover that she had very poor health. Her house was a mess, and her general appearance made her look like an accident about to happen. When she shook my hand at the end of the service, her hand was so limp I felt like handing it back to her. I would ask, "How are you?" and she would then proceed to tell me her latest tale of woe.

I was only 22 years old at the time, but I learned one lesson in a hurry. I stopped asking her how she was! Instead, I gave her my finest smile and said, calling her by name, "You look so much better. You must be feeling better."

Believe it or not, within a few months she was looking better and apparently feeling better. With the help of some friends, I dropped a seed thought into her mind that became a dominant thought. And as she thought, so she became.

What is poise?

Over time, I observed an increase in that woman's poise. You will find poise complex in its makeup. The Amplified Bible translates Philippians 4:5 as follows: "Let all men know and perceive and recognize your unselfishness (your considerateness, your forbearing spirit). The Lord is near [He is coming soon]."

The word translated "unselfishness," "considerateness," and "forbearing spirit" can also be rendered as "fairness," "reasonableness," "mildness," "patience," and "leniency." The word further carries the sense of "congeniality of spirit." All this underlies and defines the term *poise*. The person of poise is one marked by unassuming assurance, an easy dignity of manner. You may define poise as the peace of God expressed in human behavior.

How do we develop poise? There are many ways. But you will not get far unless you can take command of your mental processes. Poise, then, first requires that we exercise thought control.

Control your thoughts, control your feelings

> Whatsoever things are true, whatsoever things are honest, whatsoever things are just, whatsoever things are pure, whatsoever things are lovely, whatsoever things are of good report; if there be any virtue, and if there be any praise, think on these things (Philippians 4:8).

> As he thinketh in his heart, so is he: Eat and drink, saith he to thee; but his heart is not with thee (Proverbs 23:7).

I have already said that while we cannot control our feelings directly, we can control them indirectly by controlling our thoughts.

You can control your thoughts consciously if you want to. To be sure, it will take some discipline. Arnold Bennett, in his splendid book *How to Live on Twenty-Four Hours a Day*, challenges the reader to think on any given subject every day for at least 15 minutes without permitting his mind to wander. I challenge you to try it.

Many people can brood for 15 minutes. They can worry for 15 minutes. But very few people can focus their attention on any given (and, I might add, worthwhile) subject for 15 minutes. Almost without exception, after two minutes, their minds will have drifted onto something else.

To repeat a statement previously made in this book: You cannot have thoughts of fear and, at the same time, act courageously. If you want victory over anxiety, you must learn to control your thoughts. Only by doing this can you develop the poise that conquers worry.

We are what we think

The old saying is true. In the words of Marcus Aurelius, "A man's life is what his thoughts make of it." Ralph Waldo Emerson states that truth in another way when he says, "A man is what he thinks about all day long." Our dominant thoughts tend to externalize themselves. What lives within us sooner or later finds outward expression.

It's an old trick, but school children still love to play it. One will go to Billy and say, "You look terrible. Are you feeling well today?" A little later another child will approach Billy with a similar suggestion. And then a third. And a fourth. Soon the thought of not being well becomes Billy's dominant thought—and he goes home sick!

So take care what you let into your mind. Paul instructed us to think on things that are true. Don't think on falsehood. If you think on falsehood, soon you will act upon that which is false. As a result, your heart will condemn you and your worries will increase.

Think upon things that are honest and praiseworthy. As you do so, your thoughts will inevitably begin to externalize themselves. Think honestly, and you will live honestly. If you cannot describe something as good and honorable, then refuse to think of it at all. It will only pollute your mind and sap your resolve to win over your worries.

You also want to think upon things that are pure. As Peter said, "Gird up the loins of your mind" (1 Peter 1:13). An impure thought always precedes an impure deed. Keep your thoughts pure, and your deeds will be pure. Pure thoughts are incompatible with worrisome thoughts.

Moving on in Philippians 4:8, the apostle Paul said to think on things "of good report." The words "good report" come from two words meaning "fair speaking." The phrase could also be translated "attractive." Attractive thoughts will also deliver you from worry and being a sourpuss.

Paul then added, "If there be any virtue, and if there be any praise, think on these things." The word "virtue" comes from the Greek word *aresko*, which means "to please." Here again, learn to control your thoughts so they will relate to that which pleases. That means they will be pleasing thoughts.

With God's help, you have the power to control your thoughts. Some people unwittingly invite misery because they invite destructive thoughts into their minds. They use no discernment in the selection of the guests they invite into their minds. They think thoughts of worry, fear, and anxiety. Consequently they don't see the glass half full; rather, they always see it half empty.

They spurn the sunlight of optimism for the ominous clouds of pessimism. They come up with sanctimonious witticisms like "I expect the worst so I will never be disappointed." In a way they're right. Expect the worst, and you *will* get the worst. Thoughts of the worst dominating your life tend to externalize themselves into your outward actions, which means that your expectations become a self-fulfilling prophecy. You yourself, therefore, create a self-destroying monster.

Think for yourself

Do your own thinking. You must guard yourself even against the well-meaning but often negative and damaging advice of relatives and friends. They may mean well, but they often pull against your best interests by encouraging you to go easy on yourself.

Don't leave your mind open to the negative influence of other people. Read the biography of any dynamic personality—any achiever—and almost without exception you will discover that discouraging remarks, poor advice, negative influences, and downright opposition were thrown across his or her path by people in his or her inner circle.

Misery loves company, and you can be sure that other worriers will do their best to drag you down to their level. The following story illustrates the point well.

There were two farmers. One was a pessimist, the other was an optimist.

The optimist would say, "Wonderful sunshine."

The pessimist would respond, "Yeah, I'm afraid it's going to scorch the crops."

The optimist would say, "Fine rain."

The pessimist would respond, "Yeah, I'm afraid we are going to have a flood."

One day the optimist said to the pessimist, "Have you seen my new bird dog? He's the finest money can buy."

The pessimist said, "You mean that mutt I saw penned up behind your house? He don't look like much to me."

The optimist said, "How about going hunting with me tomorrow?"

The pessimist agreed. They went out and shot some ducks. The ducks landed on a pond. The optimist ordered his dog to get the ducks. The dog obediently responded. Instead of swimming in the water, however, the dog walked on top of the water to retrieve the ducks.

The optimist turned to the pessimist and said, "Now, what do you think of that?"

Whereupon the pessimist replied, "Hmmm, he can't swim, can he?"

In the strength of God, control your thoughts. Let them be regulated according to the will of God. Such thoughts will lead to inner poise that is a shield against worry.

11

WIN OVER WORRY
by Self-control

Fifty years ago I was invited to pastor a church of 3,000 members, which at that time was considered a large church. During my first year there, I took measures to add individuals to my staff, including an associate minister who seemed eminently qualified.

One day, during a private meeting in my office, I made a statement which, for the life of me, I cannot recall at the moment. I was seated behind my desk, and the associate minister had sat down on a divan against the far wall. He misunderstood what I was saying and took it as a personal insult.

He glowered as he warned me, "You know, I'm a former prize-fighter, and if you take this kind of an approach, I'll be forced to mop the gutter with you."

Well, that flew all over me. I could feel the blood leaving my face. I arose slowly from my chair, moved with measured and slow steps around the desk over to where he sat, grabbed him by his shirt and tie, and raised him to his feet (he was a much bigger man than I). With my index finger I poked his sternum as I said, "Throw the first punch, and your mother will be sorry she ever brought you into this world."

It was puerile. It was God-dishonoring. It was inexcusable. He was wrong in misunderstanding and threatening me, and I was inexcusably wrong in my response.

His face blanched. I am sure that given his size and experience, he could have whipped me. But at that time, neither he nor I believed it.

The next morning when I arrived at the office, I asked for him. I had endured a sleepless night, and I wanted to apologize and ask his forgiveness. He had not shown up. After some investigation, I found out he had left town at midnight with his family and had left instructions for a moving company to pack up his things and send them to a location that they would not divulge to me.

Three years passed by. During that time, every time I reflected upon that experience I grew sick inside. I knew that if I kept dwelling on what had happened, I could drop dead of a massive stroke or heart attack. My cardiovascular system simply could not tolerate the damage I was inflicting upon it. (Incidentally, two of my good friends—men of senior status and great business achievements—dropped dead in the midst of such explosions of anger.)

Three years later, after I had moved to another city, my executive assistant said, "Reverend So-and-so has phoned to see if you will accept a call from him." I said, "Of course. I've been trying to find him."

A few hours later, the call came through and my former assistant said, "I need to say something."

I interrupted him and said, "No, I must say something, and I must say it before you say a word." I then apologized to him in as complete and contrite and God-honoring a manner as I knew how. I asked for his forgiveness. I told him that the Lord had forgiven me, and I wanted his forgiveness.

It was a beautiful meeting by long-distance phone.

Since that time, my desire to honor the Lord and my passion for self-preservation have combined to throttle any tendency to explode. During the last half a century hence, I have become annoyed and irritated, but never angered like I was on that occasion and on some other occasions before it.

Had the Lord not given me victory in controlling my emotions, I believe that I would not only have disgraced the Lord, but I would have long since been dead.

Never make the mistake of retaliating

Never retaliate when others hurt you. In retaliating you may force someone to pay the price of his behavior toward you, but the cost to you will be far greater. The Bible tells us that we must love our enemies (see Matthew 5:44). As long as you go on hating your enemies, you are giving them the sovereignty of your own life. You are literally allowing them to dominate you.

For instance, imagine there is a man who has wronged you. You loathe him. Your loathing becomes a festering personality sore. You so detest him you would not welcome him into your home. You would not permit him to fraternize with your relatives. You would not invite him to eat at your table or spend the night in your guest room.

Yet all the time you are busy hating him, you are already "entertaining" him in your bloodstream, your brain cells, your nerve fibers, your muscles, and the marrow of your bones. You are giving him power over your sleep, your blood pressure, your health, your happiness. You are allowing him to destroy your body and disintegrate your effectiveness. What on earth is the good of that?

Some years ago *Life* magazine carried an article on high blood pressure. It stated the chief personality trait of people with high blood pressure is resentment.

What a price to pay for lack of self-control! Such resentment leads to paying financially through doctors' bills and medical assistance. It leads to paying emotionally through shattered nerves. You also pay through reduced efficiency, which results in decreased income. And you pay domestically through strife with family members upon whom you project your bitterness and misery.

What a price!

Learn a lesson from our Lord, in whose steps we are commanded to follow: "When he was reviled, [he] reviled not again; when he suffered, he threatened not; but committed himself to him that judgeth righteously" (1 Peter 2:23). Well did the wise Solomon say, "Better...[is] he that ruleth his spirit than he that taketh a city" (Proverbs 16:32).

Reflect for a moment upon the poise of the great Abraham Lincoln. In the anguish of his most grief-producing hours, he exercised poise. Had it not been for this quality, it is doubtful that the Civil War would have ended in victory for the Union Army. It is highly doubtful his name would have been immortalized had it not been for his magnificent ability to stay calm.

Men in Lincoln's own cabinet were disloyal to him, trying on several occasions to discredit his name. To his back they made light of him, scoffed at his limited education, and sneered at his rustic ways. Realizing that their disloyalty was to him personally, and realizing further that they possessed qualities that made them essential to our nation, the ex-railsplitter exercised self-control, disregarding the insults his colleagues heaped upon him.

Practice self-control in the face of criticism

In attaining mastery of self-control, you must learn how to conquer criticism. I do not mean that you should try to avoid criticism; you will find that impossible. Nor do I mean that you should subdue criticism—that will prove counterproductive. You can conquer it, however, by treating it in the right way.

Once again, follow the example of our Lord, who answered His critics so often with silence. Our Lord defended other people. He defended the Word of God. He defended the work of His heavenly Father. He defended little children. Yet He never defended Himself! Usually you will find it wise not to answer your critics, tempting though it may be to do so. "Answer not a fool according to his folly, lest thou also be like unto him" (Proverbs 26:4).

Ask yourself what answering criticism will achieve. Your friends don't need an answer, because you retain their confidence. Instead, listen to the criticism objectively. Don't allow yourself to become emotionally involved. Sometimes you can profit from criticism. If the criticism is just, do something about it. If the criticism is unjust, ignore it.

On the other hand, if your enemies criticize you, so what? That's what enemies do. And remember that unjust criticism is often a backhanded compliment. It often indicates that you have excited the interest, jealousy, and envy of the critic. As the old adage goes, "No one ever kicks a dead dog."

Wise words from my father

My father gave me a formula for handling criticism that I have found helpful. He said, "John, when somebody blows up at you, listen calmly with a smile on your face. When he finishes say, 'Is that all?' He will doubtlessly erupt again, but not as long nor as heatedly as before. When he is done, once again ask, 'Is that all?' Keep doing this until finally the person has nothing more to say. With exasperation he may say, 'Well, is that not enough?'

"At that point, with calmness and a smile, pull the arrow out of your quiver that most succinctly and powerfully squelches the criticism. You will have retained your poise, and you may save a friendship. On the other hand, if the criticism is just, thank him for it and ask for his advice."

Dad used this approach with great effect.

He was traveling by train from Binghamton, New York, to Philadelphia, Pennsylvania. He was seated next to a prominent Philadelphia lawyer, who engaged my father in conversation. During the conversation, the lawyer remarked on newspaper headlines. My father said, "It appears to me this development could be a fulfillment of Bible prophecy."

"I disagree," protested the lawyer with some vigor.

"You can't."

"But I certainly can. I am free, intelligent, and articulate. I certainly can disagree with you."

The lawyer was now quite worked up emotionally.

Finally, my father said, "I didn't say what it appears to *you;* I said what it appears to *me.*"

"Oh," said the lawyer.

Not satisfied to let my father win that round, as it were, the lawyer said, "Now tell me, Reverend, if Adam had never sinned, would the death of Jesus Christ on the cross have been necessary?" Though the question sounded innocent enough, the lawyer was again indulging in a brand of criticism that endeavored to put down my father.

Dad, who had been trained in law though he did not reveal that to his traveling companion, said, "I thought you were a lawyer."

"I am," said the lawyer with some force.

"Well," said my father, "are you currently practicing?"

"I am."

"Where?"

"In Philadelphia. In fact, I practice before the state supreme court."

My father said, "And in that court is it permitted to ask hypothetical questions?"

"Oh," said the lawyer, realizing that my dad had answered his challenge without answering it.

It is true that my father was winding up the lawyer a little. He did not mean to. He innocently enough made an observation as part of what appeared to be a casual and entertaining conversation. Had my father not handled the situation the way he did, the relationship could have turned sour.

When people badmouth you

In 1965, a prominent evangelist made some vicious accusations about me. Yet he did not know me that well, and he had no basis for the accusations. I was just about to pick up the phone and call him (because the Bible says that we must not allow things like this to fester) when I received a call from Wichita, Kansas, where I had held a citywide crusade in 1960.

The chairman of the committee who had set up the crusade in 1960 had been instructed to invite me to return for another citywide crusade. I told him that I was honored by the invitation to return to one of America's great cities, but that I had to decline because my schedule was full for the next three years. He then asked me if I had a recommendation. I said, "Yes," and I recommended the man who was criticizing me all over the nation.

About a week later, I received a letter from the Wichita committee, in which they asked, "Are you aware of what this fellow is saying about you? Are you sure we ought to invite him for a meeting?" I phoned the chairman and said (tongue in cheek), "Though he, unlike you and I, does not understand what a perfectly wonderful person I am, he is a capable man, a great preacher, a good evangelist, and the Lord will bless the city through his ministry."

On my recommendation, the committee invited him to come. He came. Though I never did get to see him and I never heard from him, I learned that thousands of people in the Wichita area were positively influenced by his outstanding ministry.

You find out what people really think when they're mad at you

Anyone in leadership knows that criticism goes with the job. You constantly have to make decisions, and with every decision you make, there will be someone ready to tell you what a big mistake you've made.

Church leaders probably receive more criticism than those in other professions. If the minister wears a black suit, critics will say, "Who does he think he is—Digger O'Dell?" If he wears a sport coat, the critics will question, "What is he trying to do, imitate a movie star?"

If he has five children, critics will say, "He can't afford such a family. Why doesn't he use better sense?" If he has only one child, they will quip, "Doesn't he know the Bible says that we are to be fruitful and multiply?"

If he visits the poor, they will say he is showing off. If he visits the rich, they will say he is playing politics.

If he drives an upscale car, they will say he ought to drive a car priced within his means. If he drives an economy car, they will say, "What's he trying to do, embarrass us by making people think we don't pay him enough?"

If he preaches 40 minutes, they will say he is longwinded. If he preaches 20 minutes they will ask, "What's the matter, didn't he study last week?"

If he leaves town for important speaking engagements, they will complain, "He ought to stay home and take care of the flock." If he stays home and never goes away, they will howl, "What's the matter, doesn't anyone else want him either?"

My father gave me some good advice when I entered the ministry. He said, "John, listen to what people say when they are mad. That's what they really mean."

Let's say a man flies off the handle. He says some nasty things. After he cools down he comes back and says, "I didn't really mean that." Of course he meant it! If he had not thought it, he would not have said it, for God's Word makes it clear that "out of the abundance of the heart the mouth speaketh" (Matthew 12:34). He didn't draw those words and thoughts out of thin air. They were in his heart beforehand.

While I am no disciple of psychologist Sigmund Freud, I do believe in the so-called Freudian slips. When a person writes me a letter in longhand and crosses out one word and writes down another, I have been known to spend 15 or 20 minutes holding that letter up to the light, trying to decipher the crossed-out word. In all probability, that first word was what the writer really meant.

There is another lesson here, of course. Angry criticism can arouse an angry response in you. When you answer criticism in anger, however, you risk losing possession of your faculties. Your thoughts can become inaccurate, your decisions can become unwise, and you may end up regretting your words.

How to cope at the critical moment

Let me tell you about a little habit I have formed that has served me well.

As I have admitted, by nature I am very explosive. After all, I am half-Syrian, and people from that part of the world are not famous for being phlegmatic. When God called me into the ministry, He impressed upon me the fact that by His grace my spirit must be completely dominated by Him if I wanted to be an effective ambassador of the Court of Heaven.

I memorized and meditated upon 2 Timothy 2:24-25: "The servant of the Lord must not strive; but be gentle unto all men, apt to teach, patient, in meekness instructing those that oppose themselves; if God peradventure will give them repentance to the acknowledging of the truth."

Now here is the procedure I have followed when the provocation of unjust criticism has sorely tempted me to lose my head: Through sheer conscious effort I try to listen objectively. I look at the person who is venting his anger on me. But I do not see him, for I am imagining myself as a huge elephant walking down the street. Over by the curb (and, I am sometimes inclined to think, in the gutter), a little ant is spitting at the elephant.

Ludicrous? Precisely. It helps my sense of humor. Now then, does the elephant feel threatened by the ant? Of course not. Does the elephant stop and get involved in an argument? Of course not. The elephant just serenely moves on by.

All I can say is that this certainly works for me, and I have no copyright on it. It keeps me in complete possession of my faculties so that I can think clearly and quickly, talk judiciously, and act wisely. An American statesman was once quoted as saying, "Never lose your temper, unless you do it on purpose." That's a statement worth thinking about.

Let's go back to Abraham Lincoln for just a moment. While he was an occupant of the White House, some loquacious "smut sprayers" and "character assassins" spread the rumor that he was living with a black woman. What did the president do? Nothing. This man of poise had learned that in a fight with a skunk you might win the fight, but you will smell awful afterwards!

A vital relationship with God through Christ will result naturally in self-control. When you possess self-control, you will refuse to respond to criticism with smug complacence, worldly courtesy, patronizing condescension, or vindictive retaliation. You will respond with love that is not compatible with worry-producing fear:

> There is no fear in love; but perfect love casteth out fear: because fear hath torment.
>
> He that feareth is not made perfect in love (1 John 4:18).

12

WIN OVER WORRY
by Enthusiasm

It was once my privilege to have an interview with Ray Jenkins, the brilliant lawyer from Knoxville, Tennessee, who presided over the Army-McCarthy hearings in Washington, D.C. during the 1950s. In the course of a conversation I asked him his formula for success in speaking. He mentioned several things, but one remains paramount in my mind. He said, "Don't ever speak on a subject about which you are not totally enthused."

Emotion motivates

Enthusiasm is an indispensable ingredient of poise. Some pseudointellectuals may take exception to enthusiasm and insist that we do everything on the basis of cool reason alone. I reply simply that most of what we do is done on the basis of emotional rather than intellectual impulse. I do not love my wife because of an intellectual theory about her. Rather, I love her because of an emotional impulse.

Similarly, you did not buy that insurance policy because of some fine calculation of the odds that you might die in the next five years. No doubt calculation entered your decisions, but the main inducement was strictly emotional. You saw your family destitute and in want because of inadequate material resources. It was this emotional reaction that led you to buy the insurance policy.

Or consider a football game. There, you can tell no difference in behavior between the spectator with a third-grade education and the one with several doctoral degrees. They both respond emotionally, with enthusiasm, when their team scores.

One of my hobbies is reading books on salesmanship. I have a collection of more than 50 such books. Without exception, each book on salesmanship underscores enthusiasm as an essential quality for success.

The leaders of this world have always been men and women of enthusiasm. Even Adolf Hitler knew the power of enthusiasm. His formula for speaking was, "Say it simply. Say it often. Make it burn." Thanks in part to this insight, the Austrian decorator became a world figure who could not be ignored.

Paul the apostle was a man of enthusiasm, as his own autobiographical remarks in Galatians 1:14 and Acts 22:3 attest. He was so enthusiastic about the gospel that some of the people in Corinth accused him of madness (see 2 Corinthians 5:13).

Faith and enthusiasm ought to mix

The person who never wonders at anything never does anything wonderful.

That helps to explain why the work of the Lord suffers so across the land. Thousands of people who profess a relationship with God through Jesus Christ have apparently failed to grasp what Christ has done for them and what their privileges are in Him. That's why they come to church on Sunday morning with a long face. You could ruin the greatest football team in the nation just by filling the grandstands for four consecutive games with the average Sunday morning congregation. No wonder other belief systems—such as New Age and Islam—continue to spread rapidly while the Christian faith fails to keep pace with the population increase of the world.

It's not hard to find people with a passion for movies, opera, fashion, surfboarding, or computer games. But sometimes you'd be hard put to find the same kind of emotional response to the gospel of Christ. Next Sunday when you go to church, watch the average person as he enters. He shuffles along, dragging his lower lip behind him. Then he slides into the pew and hangs his lower lip over the pew in front of him. He looks as happy as the skull and crossbones on an iodine bottle. No wonder he hasn't attracted others to Christ.

Remember: You cannot act one way and feel another. When you act sour, you become sour. Some people who profess "religion" have talked about it for so long in negative terms that those whom they influence have come to see it as a blight.

I heard about a man who walked into a hotel lobby and stood beside another man at the room clerk's counter. The fellow eyed his neighbor for a moment, and then could not restrain himself from asking, "Are you a preacher?"

"No," the other replied. "I've just been sick!"

And I can well understand the little girl who came home from Sunday school and, going up to Betsy, the mule, lovingly stroked her long head and said, "Bless you, Betsy; you must be a wonderful Christian. You look just like Grandma."

Not only is a lack of enthusiasm ruinous to the work of the Lord; it is also ruinous to happiness in the home, success in business, the making and keeping of friends, and achievement in any field.

Enthusiasm creates passion

There is no such thing as a well-adjusted personality apart from enthusiasm. There is no such thing as a satisfactory social relationship apart from enthusiasm. You reap what you sow. If you sow the wind, you will reap the whirlwind. If you sow a deadpan expression, that is exactly what others will give back to you. For what you give out you receive back in kind, only to a greater degree. That's a fact borne out by many years of observation.

As the Bible wisely says, "Whatsoever thy hand findeth to do, do it with thy might; for there is no work, nor device, nor knowledge, nor wisdom, in the grave, whither thou goest" (Ecclesiastes 9:10). Enthusiasm is like steam. It pressurizes, empowers, impels action. Many people never become enthusiastic over anything; therefore, they never achieve anything. Their lives become idle and negative and worrisome.

You know people, and so do I, who constantly complain that they don't get enough sleep. They lament that they wake up every morning feeling as tired as when they went to bed. But what happens when they plan something they really want to do—a holiday, or a fishing trip? They are awake before the alarm sounds at four o'clock in the morning—and feeling great! The explanation? Enthusiasm! All things being equal, the person who is enthusiastic turns out twice as much work as the person who is listless.

Enthusiasm is the key to career success

No great work has ever been done without enthusiasm. Look around you at the great leaders of industry, the great media figures, the great sports personalities. Without exception, they are driven by enthusiasm. They focus on the one thing that motivates them, and the power of that motivation emerges in high performance.

To be sure, some people seem to be born with a greater capacity for enthusiasm than others. But that doesn't mean you can't cultivate it. You can develop enthusiasm. Concentrate your mind on a worthwhile goal until the attainment of that goal becomes your obsession.

The salespeople who succeed vibrate with enthusiasm. Their enthusiastic belief in the product they sell turbocharges their sales. Musicians who succeed beam with enthusiasm. Who can watch a great conductor at the head of one of the world's great orchestras and not feel the enthusiasm that drives that person to prominence? I submit to you that achievement is impossible without enthusiasm.

If you go about your daily responsibilities in a listless and lackadaisical spirit, devoid of enthusiasm, I can tell you right here and now that you are doomed to mediocrity at best and failure at worst. Not only that, but your failure will create anxiety and worry, and that anxiety and worry will loop back to compound the failure and make it a permanent feature of your life. You will dig yourself into a hole.

You can be enthusiastic anywhere and in any circumstance

Remember that you cannot focus your attention upon two competing thoughts at the same time. When you are enthused, you focus your attention on positive thoughts that crowd out fears and worries. It doesn't matter how many things seem to be going wrong in your life.

See, for instance, how much the apostle Paul could have complained about:

> Of the Jews five times received I forty stripes save one. Thrice was I beaten with rods, once was I stoned, thrice I suffered shipwreck, a night and a day I have been in the deep; in journeyings often, in perils of waters, in perils of robbers, in perils by mine own countrymen, in perils by the heathen, in perils in the city, in perils in the wilderness, in perils in the sea, in perils among false brethren; in weariness and painfulness, in watchings often, in hunger and thirst, in fastings often, in cold and nakedness. Beside those things that are without, that which cometh upon me daily, the care of all the churches (2 Corinthians 11:24-28).

Did Paul worry? Did he fret? No! A godly enthusiasm delivered him from self-pity and worry. Ponder the poise he achieved through cultivating enthusiasm:

> We are troubled on every side, yet not distressed; we are perplexed, but not in despair; persecuted, but not forsaken;

cast down, but not destroyed...for which cause we faint not; but though our outward man perish, yet the inward man is renewed day by day. For our light affliction, which is but for a moment, worketh for us a far more exceeding and eternal weight of glory (2 Corinthians 4:8-9,16-17).

13

WIN OVER WORRY
by Relaxation

In the late 1970s, my young colleague, Dr. Michael Youssef, and I were waiting for the delayed takeoff of a Pan American flight from Miami to Rio de Janeiro. Our destination was Sao Paulo, where I was to lead a seminar the following day. Finally, at 11 o'clock at night, the plane started rumbling down the runway. I turned to Michael and said, "I'm going to turn on my light and do some reading."

In what seemed just moments later, I was aware that the plane was still rumbling down the runway. I turned to Michael and said, "When in the world are we going to take off?"

He replied, "This is Caracas, Venezuela. You have been sleeping so hard since we left Miami that we couldn't even shake you awake for the meal."

We stayed on the ground in Caracas for an hour. I then slept the four hours from Caracas to Rio de Janeiro. We made a quick transfer flight to Sao Paulo. I cleaned up, shaved, combed my hair. When we disembarked in Sao Paulo, I was ready for a full day's work.

Michael said, "Chief, I am willing to go anywhere with you, but next time, I'm going to leave two days early."

I said to him what I've said to people all over the world: "One of the best investments of discipline and effort you can make is in learning how to relax. Get proper rest, whether it be eight hours end to end, or six hours with snoozes throughout the day. Do whatever is the best for you, but make sure you do it." This secret had enabled me to handle a demanding global ministry. I had more stamina at age 52 than I did at age 27.

Put relaxation in your diary

Poise and relaxation go together like bread and butter or ham and eggs. You cannot maintain poise while you are tense. But by the same token, you cannot relax and worry at the same time.

Learn how to work under pressure without working under tension. This is possible if you have periodic breaks in your activities. Breaks don't have to mean inactivity. The break may simply be a change in activity. That's the way your heart works—and does your heart have to stay on the job! Did you know your heart pumps enough blood through your body every 24 hours to fill a railway tanker? Every day it exerts as much effort as it would take to shovel 20 tons of gravel onto a platform as high as your waist.

A lot of people say, "I can't relax; I've got too much to do." If you think you can attempt to excuse your tension in this way, forget it! No one has had near the responsibilities that fell upon our blessed Lord. If anyone had cause for tension, He had. Yet He always remained relaxed. Even when His enemies sought to kill Him (Luke 4:28-30). He moved quietly and unhurriedly out of their midst. Can you picture our Lord in a frenzied hurry?

Sure, Jesus took His work seriously: "I must work the works of him that sent me, while it is day: the night cometh, when no man can work" (John 9:4). But He kept His pace.

On occasions when others tried to pressure Him, Jesus said, in substance, "My opportunity is not yet come. The time is not fulfilled." Jesus Christ is our Exemplar in poise through relaxation. Hear Him as He says, "Come ye yourselves apart into a desert place, and rest a while" (Mark 6:31).

The lesson is clear: Come apart, or fall apart! It's too easy to be in a rush, driven by a relentless work schedule, and allow insufficient food, insufficient exercise, and insufficient sleep to erode your effectiveness. It's always an easy excuse to say you're busy. But being busy can boil down to a state of perpetual nervous tension—a biochemical high you can't come down from until circumstances get the better of you. Focus on results, not activity.

As the Bible reminds us:

> Don't worry over anything whatever; tell God every detail of your needs in earnest and thankful prayer, and the peace of God, which transcends human understanding, will keep constant guard over your hearts and minds as they rest in Christ Jesus (Philippians 4:6 PHILLIPS).

Finding your rhythm can double your effectiveness

There is a rhythm, a cadence, in all of nature. Plants reproduce themselves in their seasons, and human beings in their generations. There is a rhythm, a cadence, in all the actions of nature: in our breathing, in the ebbing and flowing of the tide, in the rising and setting of the sun. One of the earmarks of an amateur musician is that he or she does not give proper attention to the rests.

Apparently Thomas Edison got by on four hours of sleep a day. However, he had the ability to "snooze" at almost any hour of the day or night. He was relaxed at all times.

When I was a young man I read a line by New York psychologist Dr. David Seabury that impelled me to look at this matter seriously. He wrote that we need rest for the body and sleep for the mind. He went on to say that the man who stays free of psychic tensions gets by on less sleep than the man who gets tied up in knots.

The last year that Dr. Robert G. Lee served as president of the Southern Baptist Convention (the world's largest Protestant denomination), he was in his late sixties. During that year he traveled over 150,000 miles and oversaw the building of an auditorium that cost more than $21 million in 2009 dollars. He also received over 1,200 new members into the 9,000-member Bellevue Baptist Church in Memphis, Tennessee, of which he was pastor.

One of his members, a prominent Memphis surgeon, Dr. J. Murray Davis, told me that the secret of Dr. Lee's output was his capacity to relax. Dr. Davis said, "It is incredible how this man maintains such a pace despite his years." Then the surgeon recounted this incident from the life of Dr. Lee:

> One Sunday morning I went to make my hospital visits at six o'clock. Dr. Lee was also at the hospital visiting. He then taught our Sunday school class later that morning and followed that by the delivery of one of his matchless sermons at the 11 o'clock hour. Immediately after the morning service he flew by chartered plane to Longview, Texas, where he delivered a baccalaureate address in the afternoon. He flew back to Memphis in time to speak at a special assembly of the Baptist Training Union in our church. Following that he delivered the evening message at the 7:30 evangelistic hour. After the benediction of the evening service he rushed to the airport, where he boarded a plane for California. He flew all night and spoke Monday evening to a large convocation in California.

What a pace! And remember, he was at an age when many folks have already retired.

For more than a quarter of a century Dr. Lee averaged 11 visits a day. He preached in his own church a minimum of three times a week and he taught a Sunday school class 44 Sundays out of every year. After he turned 40 years of age, he built a church from a membership of 1,300 to more than 9,000—all the while traveling and preaching outside his own city and preaching nearly as often as an evangelist.

The secret? He knew how to relax. He knew how to pace himself. He worked under pressure without working under tension.

Relaxation helps older people hyperperform

Learn the rhythm of successful living. When you work, work. When you rest, rest.

When my father was 62 years of age he pastored a vigorous church in the state of New York. He slept only a few hours a night. He walked two miles a day. He was one of the best paddleball players in Binghamton, New York, and all his opponents were under 35 years of age. On his sixtieth birthday he played two sets of tennis. How did he do it? He knew how to relax.

On several occasions, when I visited my father, he would be sitting in his high-back rocking chair. Right in the middle of our conversation he would say, "You must excuse me, son. I am going to take a few minutes' snooze." He would set his head back and sleep for perhaps seven minutes, then open his eyes again, fresh and alert, and say, "All right, now. Where were we?"

Most great achievers maintain the practice of having a nap sometime during the day. It has been proven that a person will fare better with six hours of sleep at night and an hour of sleep every afternoon than with eight hours of sleep at night and no break during the day.

As a young man I realized that if I was going to be productive, I would have to master the ability to relax and sleep. I worked at it assiduously. In the late 1960s, I boarded a flight from Seattle to Tokyo. Then-head of World Vision, Dr. Ted Engstrom, was on the same flight. He said, "John, people tell me that you can sleep like a baby on these flights, and you don't even take a sleeping pill. I don't believe it."

I grinned and said, "Well, Ted, I'm grateful to God. It's true."

Our flight lifted off. We had a meal, after which I read a paper and thumbed through a magazine. About an hour and a half out of Seattle,

I stretched across the three seats and laid my head on three pillows just under the window. I slept soundly until half an hour outside of Tokyo. Ted couldn't believe it.

There's no way that I could have maintained my schedule over the past 40 years had I not learned the secret of relaxation. In that time, I have made 103 trips around the world; written 15 books and hundreds of inches of copy for brochures, appeal letters, and magazine articles; averaged a speech nearly once a day; administrated an organization with offices on every inhabited continent; and maintained my personal study habits and responsibilities.

Were it not for my ability to relax, I would have become a physical and emotional basket case by now. At an age that some consider 20 years past retirement, I thank God I'm still able to function with a great deal of energy and zest. The key? The ability to relax.

Relaxation is a vital component of poise. The soil of tension and frenzy will produce long green shoots of worry in your life. Therefore, ask God to help you find poise through relaxation.

14

WIN OVER WORRY
by Scheduling

During the 1970s, Korean Presbyterians invited me to be the evangelist for the Seventh Decade Spiritual Revolution Crusade. The chairman of that event was Dr. Kyung Chik Han, pastor of the world's largest Presbyterian church—the Young Nak (meaning "eternal joy") Church in Seoul. The evangelistic effort lasted for three weeks, with one week being spent in each of three cities—Pusan, Taegu, and Seoul.

For 21 days I was honored to be in the company of this distinguished world leader. Twice dispossessed of all—literally *all*—his earthly goods, Dr. Han had known the scourge of Japan's cruel occupation in the 1940s and North Korea's atheistic terrorism in the 1950s.

What I learned from Dr. Han

In 1956, along with 27 North Korean refugees, Dr. Han founded the Young Nak Church. Just after the outer structure of the new sanctuary was completed, North Koreans stormed across the 38th parallel and into Seoul, driving freedom-loving Koreans southward and nearly into the sea. The new sanctuary was used by the North Koreans as an ammunition depot.

Dr. Han and his people established three other Young Nak churches during their southern exile. When they returned to Seoul in 1953 the work continued, and the statistics staggered the Christian world. The membership climbed to more than 16,000 by 1972. More than 100 daughter churches were established. In addition, Dr. Han and his colleagues founded schools, orphanages, senior citizens' quarters, summer camps, spiritual retreat grounds and facilities, and special ministries among the military groups. Such was the quality of Dr. Han's leadership.

Yet the dear man never appeared harried or hurried. I watched for three weeks for any sign of pique or impatience. I never saw it. Dr. Han met with his people every morning at 5:00 for a one-hour prayer meeting. What a way to start every day!

Dr. Han's life was a model of quiet achievement for Christ. He was the master teacher of the stewardship of time. I have heard him lecture on the subject. Better, I have watched him put his teaching into practice. He so scheduled his time—so planned his work and worked his plan—that he could discharge Herculean responsibilities.

Dr. Han knew God had given him adequate time to achieve all that lay within the divine will for his work in Korea. In complete dependence upon the Holy Spirit of God, he moved peacefully and productively. Consistently relaxed and gracious, he infused this mood upon all those who worked with him.

Dr. Han's life was a symphony of poise. The atmosphere of his home made it a vestibule of heaven. Fellowship with this man of God bestowed its own special benediction.

Hurry doesn't pay

Life in the twenty-first century grows ever more frenetic. Fast travel, mobile phones, and email have made us far more accessible than we used to be. We move faster. We do more. There is more to do. And it is very easy to lose your poise under the pressure of work.

By scheduling your activities, you will make great strides toward victory in this area. Scheduling defeats frenzy and hurry. It does this by bringing regularity into lifestyle and by imposing order on what otherwise might be a chaotic, moment-to-moment existence. Hurry is symptomatic of a weakly organized mind. Without scheduling and organization you will move fast and make mistakes, and that will lead to discouragement and tension.

Let me suggest that you read the autobiography of Benjamin Franklin. He tells of his effort to master 13 virtues. He was past 80 years of age when he wrote the autobiography, and at this milestone he was forced to admit that order was the one virtue he had never been able to conquer. It is probably one of the most difficult habits to perfect.

Yet order is so important.

There is a story told of attempted escapes at a state psychiatric hospital in Illinois. One day one of the patients ran out of the gate and down the road as fast as he could run. The orderlies chased him, caught him, and brought him back. The next day another patient did exactly the same thing with the same result. That happened ten successive days with ten different patients. Now, if the ten patients had fled at the same time, and if each had run in a different direction, probably nine of them would have escaped. The lack of coordinated effort frustrated their plans.

Plan your work and work your plan

Ask God for the wisdom to help you plan your work, then ask Him for the grace to let you work your plan. The Lord is near, so call upon Him for the needed wisdom and grace.

God led Nehemiah to plan for the rebuilding of Jerusalem's walls. He led Nehemiah in the seemingly impossible feat of organizing laborers and resources to achieve the task in the teeth of unspeakable opposition. In the same way, the Lord will enable you, if you will but call upon Him, to so plan your work and work your plan that you will fulfill the divine injunction to be "always abounding in the work of the Lord" (1 Corinthians 15:58).

Fatigue is caused mostly by boredom. When you have no order—when you have failed to schedule your activities—you lack the awareness of accomplishment. Conversely, when you have wisely scheduled your activities under the leadership of the Holy Spirit, and when you are performing your responsibilities on schedule, you get a natural lift. There is nothing more invigorating than the awareness of tasks efficiently completed, and there is nothing more dispiriting than the knowledge of unfulfilled responsibilities.

List your tasks at the start of the day. As you complete them, check them off. And when you reach the end of your workday, you will experience the satisfaction of five, ten, fifteen, or twenty tasks successfully accomplished.

Paul encourages us to be "redeeming the time, because the days are evil" (Ephesians 5:16). By God's grace and in His strength, we will fulfill our responsibility to redeem the time. In doing that we will conquer worry through poise by scheduling.

The Lord gives us the ability and the time to do everything He expects us to do. We have an obligation—and a privilege—to utilize these God-given resources so that His will for us may be fulfilled. And in turn, that fulfillment honors Him and dispels anxiety. God help us to live in such a way—as our Lord while yet on earth was able to do—so that we can say, "I have finished the work which thou gavest me to do" (John 17:4).

15

WIN OVER WORRY
by Variety

In 1993, the film director Derek Jarman released a full-length movie in which the screen remained a consistent shade of blue from beginning to end. It was called—you guessed it—*Blue*. Although some critics praised the film, sitting in a movie theatre and looking at a blue screen for the entire length of a movie is just not very exciting. It's also painful on the eyes.

We were made for variety. We thrive on it. And as in filmmaking, so in conversation. People whose talk is in only one color do not command respect from others or attract their interest. The proverb: "Variety is the spice of life" remains true.

Paul had interests outside the gospel

Does it seem almost blasphemous to suggest Paul had interests outside the gospel? How could Paul, the great apostle, who was so consumed with his evangelistic mission, possibly have taken an interest in anything else?

Yet he clearly did. The apostle Paul was not only a preacher; he was also a logician. Apparently he was also interested in athletics because he alluded to sports many times in his epistles. Furthermore, his reference to Greek poets in Acts 17 suggests he was conversant with poetry.

Certainly no one can deny that Paul was also a master at understanding human nature. And his interests did not detract from his mission. Rather, they made him more able to communicate what really mattered: the good news of salvation in Christ.

Similarly, King David was a sportsman, a poet, a musician, a militarist, and a philosopher. And who could adequately evaluate the multiplicity of interests maintained by his son, Solomon?

> He spake three thousand proverbs: and his songs were a thousand and five. And he spake of trees, from the cedar tree that is in Lebanon even unto the hyssop that springeth out of the wall: he spake also of beasts, and of fowl, and of creeping things, and of fishes (1 Kings 4:32-33).

You will see from this that Solomon was a sage, a musician, a poet, a horticulturist, an expert in animal husbandry, an ornithologist, an entomologist, and a piscatologist. Presumably, had he not been good company, the Queen of Sheba would not have come from a long distance to meet him.

Or take the example of our Lord. Study His parables, and you will conclude that He knew not only what went on in the depths of the human heart, but what kinds of lives the people around Him lived. Because He was so well grounded in these things, Jesus could talk easily with men and women of every social and ethnic background. All listened to Him with interest. He appealed to the educated Nicodemus just as much as He did to the common fishermen and the woman of ill repute from Samaria.

Possessing a diversity of interests helps you to keep a balance essential to poise. It helps give you a sense of perspective and assists with communication. And it equips you with a wealth of experience, which is one of the gifts God has given humankind.

The Bible shows us that such interests should be actively cultivated. For example, when Paul was forced out of Berea by persecution, he did not go to Athens and brood. He kept busy. In Athens he went to the marketplace and listened to the dialogues of the philosophers. He studied the habit patterns of the Athenians. There he discovered what interested and motivated them.

This study quickly bore fruit. It wasn't long before the Athenians insisted Paul go to Areopagus, to the top of Mars Hill, where only the great orators and the celebrities were permitted to speak. There he delivered the most masterful sermon ever preached by any man— our Lord excepted, of course. An interest in life's variety provided the content of Paul's communication.

No one can maximize their honor of God when their interests lie within the boundaries of a narrow and specialized field. Without a variety of interests, you will not keep anyone's attention for long.

Variety keeps you balanced—even in the pulpit

I know from my own experience that the pressures on clergy are phenomenal. They are on call 24 hours a day, 7 days a week. They never have the satisfaction of knowing that everything is done. There is always another person to visit, another letter to write, another message to prepare.

In addition, they are the CEOs of their organizations, handling any number of sensitive interpersonal issues and maintaining not only a paid staff, but a large body of volunteer leaders and workers. No wonder an article published in the American press was titled "Why Ministers Are Cracking Up."

Time and again, I have seen that great ministers in tough pastorates not only survive but empower their ministries by keeping other interests alive. For example, the brilliant pulpit orator from Louisiana, Dr. James W. Middleton, went through enough tribulations to shatter the nerves of five rugged men. In the midst of his metropolitan ministry a serious throat condition requiring surgery put him out of his pulpit for nearly a year. This setback put his entire ministry in jeopardy. Yet he returned to scale new heights in the proclamation of God's Word—a feat explained in no small measure by the broad base of his interests, which included horticulture, hunting, and fishing.

Dr. Roy O. McClain, former pastor of the First Baptist Church of Atlanta, Georgia, and selected in 1957 by *Time* magazine as one of the ten most outstanding American clergymen of that year, seemed to spend every spare hour honing his powers as a speaker and communicator. Yet he had several hobbies, among which were the raising of Shetland ponies, painting, the playing of the organ, and woodworking. He found these hobbies essential. They served as a balance wheel, giving him unruffled poise as he led what was, at the time, the largest congregation in Georgia.

It's never too late to start

For years I looked with envy on people who did downhill skiing. I wanted to learn how to ski, but I felt I could not afford the expense, and I knew without a shadow of a doubt, I could not afford the time. However, I finally decided to set a goal to take up skiing at age 63. On my sixty-third birthday I flew to Germany and drove with Mr. John Bolten to Hopfgarten, Austria. For the next two-and-a-half weeks, I enjoyed the professional excellence of Austria's proverbial ski geniuses.

After seven days of learning, I was able to ski down the steepest slope of Hopfgarten Mountain. Before I left, my Austrian friends gave me a videotape made by Austria's Department of Ski Instruction so that during the summer months I could rehearse the various moves featured in the video.

This was the first time I had engaged in an athletic sideline to which I devoted any serious energy, enthusiasm, and resources. I tell you frankly that it proved as effective in undergirding my inner poise and serenity as anything I have ever done. My friend and ski companion, Hank Bronson, a Chicago businessman, served as an ideal example for me. He knows how to relax while leading a major business.

Also, you cannot come down a steep ski slope and think about anything else except skiing. It's a marvelous way to force yourself to brush aside the multitude of energy-sapping little problems that confront you when you reach the office or pick up the morning post.

Now, I'm not suggesting that you take up the same pursuit. I am suggesting that you find some equivalent activity to which you can give wholehearted enthusiasm—a hobby that helps you to relax and that reinforces inner poise. It may be cooking. Or theatre. Or plunging down flooded ravines in a rubber raft. It doesn't have to be complex or expensive. What matters is that you do it.

Work and play can be the same thing

For some people, variety seems to mean coming home from work and plopping into a chair in front of the television. In truth, they are not getting much out of the riches life can offer them.

Avoid passivity like the plague. In Mark 6:31, when Jesus said to the apostles, "Come ye yourselves apart…and rest a while," they did not lie down under an olive tree and sleep. Rather, they went out to eat, and then they engaged in a different form of activity. Variety means finding other outlets for expression, not switching yourself off. Jesus was always busy about His Father's business; He just varied the mode of His activity.

The world-famed industrialist R.G. LeTourneau once had an important appointment in his plant at Toccoa, Georgia. While in flight to Georgia, the pilot of LeTourneau's plane discovered that the landing gear was stuck. The pilot radioed ahead to the airport personnel in Anderson, South Carolina, and told them the problem. Ambulances and a rescue squad rushed to the airport. The news media arrived to cover the event. The plane made a good crash landing.

But when LeTourneau got out of the plane, his first words had nothing to do with what had just happened. He said, in substance, "Where's the car? I am already late for my appointment in Toccoa. Can you get me a car immediately?"

That is poise.

I once asked LeTourneau when he took his vacation. He said, "I never take a vacation. My work is my play and you never need a vacation from play." There was a man who, through Christ and wise self-discipline, learned the poise that conquers worry.

16

WIN OVER WORRY
by Seizing the Day

Yesterday is a cashed check and cannot be negotiated. Tomorrow is a promissory note and cannot yet be utilized. Today is cash in hand. Spend it wisely.

The songwriter D.W. Whittle understood this truth when in 1893 he wrote:

> Moment by moment I'm kept in His love;
> Moment by moment I've life from above:
> Looking to Jesus till glory doth shine;
> Moment by moment, O, Lord, I am thine.

The trouble with many people is that instead of looking to Jesus they are looking to tomorrow, waiting for circumstances to turn and favor them. What a tragic waste of opportunity. The psalmist tells us, "This is the day which the LORD hath made; we will rejoice and be glad in it" (Psalm 118:24). Global radio broadcaster Lowell Thomas had these words framed and hung in his broadcasting studio at his farm so that he could see them often. If the conviction of your heart is summed up in this verse, it is impossible for you to worry.

There is no point in living in the past. Paul was in the habit of "forgetting those things which are behind" (Philippians 3:13). All your opportunities and responsibilities lie right here in the present. So give every moment your all. Give your entire attention to the work at hand, the person with whom you are talking or dealing. The Lord grants us time only here and now. You can use each moment only once.

God will give you what you need today

Many people say, "If only this or that would change, then I could reach my goals."

Nonsense! God gives you today exactly what you need today.

The Bible illustrates this principle perfectly in relation to the manna God gave to the children of Israel while they were in the wilderness. Read the passage:

> This is the thing which the LORD hath commanded, Gather of it every man according to his eating, an omer for every man, according to the number of your persons…And the children of Israel did so, and gathered, some more, some less. And when they did mete it with an omer, he that gathered much had nothing over, and he that gathered little had no lack; they gathered every man according to his eating. And Moses said, Let no man leave of it till the morning. Not-withstanding they hearkened not unto Moses; but some of them left of it until the morning, and it bred worms, and stank (Exodus 16:16-20).

The Israelites needed food. They needed it today, tomorrow, and the day after that.

But the Lord provided for them a daily supply. He did not send down manna in seven-day sacks. If anyone gathered more than he or she needed for the day, all the excess rotted. The truth is simply this: God's sustenance comes to you now, right at this moment. You cannot have this day again, so you must make the best job of it you can. Whatever God wants you to do today, He has given you the resources to do—today!

Jesus lived and worked in the "now"

Here again our Lord is the example. He came to earth to die. His death and resurrection made it possible for Him to set up a kingdom—a kingdom not of this world, but a spiritual kingdom. Said Jesus, "To this end was I born, and for this cause came I into the world" (John 18:37).

The shadow of persecution and death constantly lay across Jesus' path. Yet He lived one day at a time and did not permit the grief, torture, and pain that faced Him to rob Him of perfect composure for today. Little children reveled in His company. Men who conversed with Him were aware of His total concern over their problems. Our Lord even said, "My hour is not yet come." In other words, He lived moment by moment, one day at a time. Observe His matchless poise!

Don't be forever living in the future. It's true that as a Christian, you are to look unceasingly for the blessed hope and glorious appearing of Jesus Christ (see Titus 2:13). But as you do so, don't neglect your present work. Live in such a way that you will never be ashamed to meet Jesus, whenever He appears.

In Acts 1:6 the followers of our Lord asked, "Lord, wilt thou at this time restore again the kingdom to Israel?" Consider the answer our Lord gave: "It is not for you to know the times or the seasons, which the Father hath put in his own power. But ye shall receive power, after that the Holy Ghost is come upon you" (Acts 1:7-8).

Our Lord replied by showing the disciples that the finest possible preparation they could make for the future was a Spirit-led execution of the present. The proof that the child of God is looking forward to the second coming of Christ is his faithfulness in living today for the glory of God.

The *Today Principle* is widely applied

The French philosopher and writer Michel de Montaigne said, "My life has been full of terrible misfortunes, most of which never happened." Many of us might say the same thing. How foolish of us to scuttle our opportunities and waste the privileges of this day, which is slipping away with fantastic speed.

John Ruskin had on his desk a simple piece of stone on which was chiseled one word: TODAY.

The physician and author Sir William Osler gives good advice when he says, "Banish the future; live only for the hour and its allotted work…Set earnestly at the little task at your elbow…our plain duty is, 'Not to see what lies dimly at a distance, but to do what lies clearly at hand.' "

Yes, seize today! The minister Richard Baxter left to us sage advice when he said, "Spend your time in nothing which you know must be repented of; in nothing on which you might not pray for the blessing of God; in nothing which you could not review with a quiet conscience on your dying bed; in nothing which you might not safely and profitably be found doing if death should surprise you in the act."

Most of your misery is left over from yesterday or borrowed from tomorrow. In the dynamic of the Holy Spirit, determine to live today to the glory of God. Remember: This is the day that the Lord has made. Paul urges you to redeem the time, for the days are evil (Ephesians 5:16). God has given you today. He has taken back all your yesterdays and all your tomorrows are still in His keeping.

Living in the "now" for 24 years

I told earlier of how the Lord graciously blessed us with a precious son.

One of the nation's most respected gynecologists and obstetricians brought him into the world. Tragically, this man—overcome by grief in his life—sought to find the answer in a bourbon bottle rather than in the blessed Bible. Due to the doctor's intoxication at the time of delivery, several of our baby's bones were broken. One of his legs was pulled out at the growing center. Needless abuse—resulting in hemorrhaging of the brain—was inflicted upon the little fellow.

During the first year of his life, eight doctors said he could not possibly survive. Until he was two, my wife had to feed him every three hours with a Brecht feeder. It took a half hour to prepare for the feeding, and it took another half hour to clean up and put him back to bed. Not once during that time did she get out of the house for any diversion whatsoever. Never did she get more than two hours sleep at one time.

My wife, formerly Christine Barker of Bristol, Virginia, had once been acclaimed by some of the nation's leading musicians as one of the outstanding contemporary female vocalists in America. From the time she was 13 she had been popular as a singer—and constantly in the public eye. Hers was the experience of receiving and rejecting some fancy offers with even fancier incomes to marry an aspiring Baptist pastor with not even a church to his name!

Then, five years into our marriage, this tragedy struck. The whole episode was so unnecessary. From a life of public service, Christine was now marooned within the walls of our home. Her beautiful voice no longer enraptured public audiences with the story of Jesus, but was now silenced, or at best, muted to the subdued humming of lullabies.

Had it not been for Christine's spiritual maturity, whereby she laid hold of the resources of God and lived one day at a time, this heartrending experience would long since have caused an emotional breakdown.

John Edmund, Jr., our little son, lived 24 years and died in 1975. We rejoice that he committed his heart and life to Jesus Christ and gave evidence of a genuine concern for the things of the Lord. I attribute his commitment to Jesus Christ and his wonderful disposition to the sparkling radiance of an emotionally mature, Christ-centered mother who had mastered the discipline of living in the now.

The people who know Christine concur that, after enduring a grief more intense than most could guess, she still possesses a sparkle that would be the envy of any high school senior, and a radiance and charm for which any debutante would gladly give a fortune.

Don't let others seize the day for you

Seize the day. Live for today. Wring it dry of every opportunity. You have troubles? So do others. So did Paul, who said, "Most gladly therefore will I rather glory in my infirmities, that the power of Christ may rest upon me" (2 Corinthians 12:9).

You seize the day—don't let others seize it for you. Don't let others pressure you and shape the way you spend your time. Don't let others occupy you in wasteful socializing or activities.

If you want to socialize, if it contributes to your social well-being without imposing counterproductive pressures on you, go to it. However, I am appalled at the excessive and superficial socializing and unproductive activities in which otherwise free people allow themselves to become enslaved. They permit their minds to be divided between asking, "Is this what I ought to do?" and "What will they think of me if I don't go?" Take control of your life. Go or don't go. But don't sit on the fence.

Because so many allow themselves to become enslaved to superficial socializing or activities, they never read a book, memorize a poem, or take that course at the university night school they had promised themselves they were going to take. In short, they rob themselves of the really important contributions to their lives and influence.

Seize the day for your children

Unfortunately, our society has developed two extreme types of parents: those who abuse their children, and those who become hostage to them. In both cases, I can assure you that the major reason is the divided mind. And in both cases, the children suffer.

Let's take the case of the parents who become hostage to their children. They don't want their children to walk from the front door to the pantry. They must drive them there! Jogging for fitness is in. But for children, walking is out. These parents are determined that, whatever the cost, they are to be a spectator at every activity in which the child has a part. Consequently, we have had a 50-percent increase in obesity among children in the past ten years in the United States. The medical profession unanimously attributes this to too much television and too little exercise.

How many children do you know today who are required to do chores? Even to make their beds, help wash the dishes or the car, take care of the lawn, or assist with the housecleaning? I submit to you that in many cases, the parents have split their minds between what they know they ought to do and what their peers are doing down the street.

I was in a vigorous and enjoyable debate with a man from Yorkshire, England. He said, "When I visit your country, I am appalled that so many can't make up their minds."

"What are you talking about?" I protested.

"I'll give you a perfect illustration: Junior asks his mother if he can go to a certain function. His mother then gets on the phone and calls the mothers of all of Junior's neighbors to find out what they are going to do. After having taken a poll of the neighbors, his parents then give Junior the verdict. What a terrible way to rear a lad. They are creating an atmosphere of indecision that is bound to have a negative effect on the boy."

I protested vigorously, but in my mind I knew that—more often than I cared to admit—what he said was true.

And why do people act in this manner? The divided mind. It's divided between their responsibility as parents and their fear of falling out of line with their peers. In short, they don't seize the day. They let the day—and their peers—seize them. And that does not make for good mental health, good emotional stability, or a serene home life.

You develop greater poise when you determine to take time by the forelock and, under the leadership of God, shake it into obedience and make it your servant instead of your master.

Health is yet another area in which people become hostage to the day instead of seizing the day. A friend told me of his mother, who worried for 40 years that she would die of cancer. She died at age 73—from pneumonia. It's tragic. She wasted 40 years worrying about the wrong thing. Over those 40 years she brought depression instead of delight to the hearts of her closest friends and members of her family. For 40 years she divided her mind and her time between useful pursuits and worrying about cancer. For 40 years her testimony and witness for Christ was diminished simply because she refused to live one day at a time—and to live that day to the fullest and to the glory of God.

Read it again: "This is the day which the LORD hath made; we will rejoice and be glad in it" (Psalm 118:24).

Stop worrying about yesterday and tomorrow. Make the most of today, and rejoice in it.

17

WIN OVER WORRY
by Skill

The preacher M.E. Dodd once said, "Many are twisting a tune out of a hand organ when they ought to be playing a four-manual pipe organ. Many are satisfied to play with mud pies when they ought to be making angel food cakes. Many are crawling when they ought to be running. Many are building shacks when they ought to be building palaces."

It's true. If you want to develop the poise that conquers worry, then do everything you do the best you can and learn to master some skill.

First Corinthians 10:31 says, "Whether therefore ye eat, or drink, or whatsoever ye do, do all to the glory of God." Therefore if we are going to glorify God, we must do our best. There is no room for mediocrity in the life of the child of God. God deserves and demands our best.

> Hear ye the Master's call, "Give Me thy best!"
> For, be it great or small, that is His test.
> Do then the best you can, not for reward,
> Not for the praise of men, but for the Lord.
>
> Wait not for men to laud, heed not their slight;
> Winning the smile of God brings its delight!

Aiding the good and true ne'er goes unblest,
All that we think or do, be it the best.

Night soon comes on a pace, day hastens by:
Workman and work must face testing on high.
Oh, may we in that day find rest, sweet rest,
Which God has promised those who do their best.

Skill is essential to poise

The speaker who has subjected himself to rigorous discipline until he has perfected the craft of speaking is poised when he speaks. The speaker who has not paid the price of discipline, and who comes to the pulpit or to the lectern half-prepared, lacks poise—and if he has any discernment, he will be tortured to reflect on the mess he has made of his presentation.

The anxiety caused by lack of preparation is totally unnecessary and can be eliminated simply by paying the price to develop the needed skill. This is true no matter what a person's occupation: a doctor, a lawyer, a salesperson, an artisan, an athlete, an artist, a cook. For a professing Christian to do less than his best is inexcusable because he or she has the resources to achieve true mastery.

It is tragic that there are so few truly great musicians today. So few great orators. So few great financiers. So few great inventors. Thank God, however, that there are still some who are willing to soar to the heights of an eagle, though they know they will fly alone. For the glory of God and for their own peace of mind, they are willing to exert themselves to the full and to climb the ladder of achievement to the topmost rung.

Some time ago I had an interview with one of the greatest speech professors in America. He showed me seven pages of elementary voice exercises, which, to my amazement, he said he had practiced daily for 40 years. This man cannot tolerate mediocrity.

The great pianist Ignacy Paderewski practiced simple finger exercises for hours every day over a period of years. No wonder he could mesmerize the musical world and indeed, the man in the street, with his matchless skill.

Thomas Edison experimented hundreds of times before he successfully developed the electric light filament. While he was working on it, a scientist in England went on record as saying that the electric light filament was an impossibility, and anyone who said otherwise was a fraud. But Edison, who loathed mediocrity, kept on giving his best until success crowned his efforts.

Puritan minister Matthew Henry worked hours every day for 40 years in producing his Bible commentaries. Today, more than 300 years later, his Bible commentary set is still very popular and owned by many clergyman. Why? Because, under God, Matthew Henry gave his best.

Jesus told a parable about a man who started building a house but never lived in it (Luke 14:28-30). Our Master scorned a task half done.

For years, William Jennings Bryan unrelentingly and laboriously practiced the art of oratory. He never won a speech contest. Nevertheless he kept on. As a comparative unknown he attended the Democratic National Convention held at the Coliseum in Chicago in 1896. It was past midnight. The people were weary. Many of them were leaving. He stepped up to the stand and delivered his famous Cross of Gold oration.

This speech, so masterfully delivered by a man who never won a speech contest, catapulted Bryan into the position of standard-bearer for the Democratic Party. In less than 24 hours he had become a national figure. This mighty man of God had mastered the mechanics of the work for which God had called him, and the record of his life is a glittering trophy and an imposing monument to the glory of God.

Too often we just don't try hard enough

Peace of mind depends upon our awareness of divine approval. And there is no poise like the poise that accompanies mastery of a skill in the power of God. When we fail to give God our best, we fail to bring maximum honor and glory to His name. Consciousness of this failure produces anxiety and inner conflict.

Whatever your personal view of television, I think you must agree that the skill level of actors and performers presents one of the most stinging rebukes to the apathy of church leadership. Actors and performers will work day and night to attain mastery in the field of show business.

Singer Kate Smith dominated television when I was a younger man. I learned that for every hour she appeared on the screen, she spent 18 hours in preparation. At that time she was broadcasting five hours a week. For five hours of TV entertainment, she willingly worked 90 hours to bring to her viewers the finest programs she was capable of producing. She did not have to do this for monetary reasons, for at the time she was reputedly a millionaire several times over.

When it comes to giving our best, Christians have no excuses. In Philippians 4:13 Paul wrote, "I can do all things through Christ which strengtheneth me." You have the resources necessary to do what God requires of you. And as you fulfill His calling, you will gain the poise that conquers anxiety.

Learn to do at least one thing better than anyone else can do it

It's true of us all that we like to do what we know we can do well. The high school boy enjoys most the sport he plays best. The teacher feels most confident and comfortable in the subject area she loves and in which she has extensive knowledge.

You are less likely to worry if you feel in command of what you are doing. Worry results from a divided mind. When you are doing what you like to do, your mind is occupied with one thing. "This one thing I do," said Paul (Philippians 3:13). Dwight L. Moody added that most people today would have to change this and say, "These fifty things I dabble in."

The legendary conductor Leonard Bernstein used to do children's shows on television. For one solid hour he would hold a capacity studio audience of hundreds of children spellbound and charm millions of television viewers. He was totally absorbed in what he was doing. Obviously he enjoyed it. Why? Because he was probably the world's greatest music teacher when it came to explaining music to the masses. He liked to do this because he had mastered the skill of doing it well. At the conclusion of the hour, television viewers could detect that Bernstien was nearly exhausted but supremely happy. He was poised.

Have you not seen this happen yourself? Perhaps it was at a party, or maybe a picnic, that you saw someone who seemed absolutely disengaged from the proceedings, moping around on the sidelines and refusing to participate in the activities. Then a game or a sport was proposed, and the mention of it brought light into this person's eyes. He threw himself into that game or sport with everything he had. He was clearly skillful in that activity. And because he was doing something he knew how to do, his body became vibrant. His face shone. His conversation became animated and enthusiastic.

In short, he began to show all the evidence of being poised. His skill in the particular activity allowed him to become congenially involved in the group. His mind was no longer divided. His interests were no longer diffused. He had found his place because he could use a skill he had mastered better than anyone else there.

The satisfaction of a skill employed

When Bedan Mbugua of Kenya attended our course on advanced Christian leadership in Singapore, he was a pharmaceutical salesman. Suddenly, however, an idea struck him. He envisioned the possibility of publishing a magazine that would communicate the gospel of Jesus Christ to people who might never come to church or be interested in religious things.

When he returned to Kenya, he pursued his goal. In less than three years, the magazine he was producing outsold *Time* and *Newsweek* in five African nations, including Nigeria. He later transferred the ownership and production of the magazine to another party, and started yet another publication.

Bedan's story has been one of ever-increasing successes. He loves the work. And he loves it for one reason: because he's good at it. Equally, you could say that he's good at it because he loves it!

I repeat, we like to do what we know how to do well. Bedan Mbugua understands magazine publishing. He not only understands the writing needs, the editorial needs, and the demographics of the areas where he intends to sell, but he also understands the business aspects, marketing techniques, and all of the various elements essential to the production of an influential magazine.

If you want to conquer worry, discipline yourself to the point of mastery in the field to which God has called you. For your own peace of mind, excel in at least one thing. Gather your resources, rally all your faculties, marshal all your energies, and focus all your capacities upon mastery in at least one field of endeavor.

This is a surefire antidote to the divided mind. Stop scattering your efforts. Cease halfhearted attempts to be superb at everything. Ascertain the will of God for your life. Enlist His help and strength, and trust that through Him you can do all things. Strive for mastery, and soon you will experience worry-killing poise as a result of your skill.

18

WIN OVER WORRY
by Industry

The person who said, "I've found a great way to start the day—I go straight back to bed" was very sadly mistaken. Idleness subjects you to destructive thoughts, dangerous impulses, and perilous pressures from without. All these things contribute to anxiety.

Jesus Himself said, "I must work" (John 9:4). He also said, "My Father worketh hitherto, and I work" (John 5:17). Work is divine in its inception. The old adage "Idleness is the devil's workshop" is true.

Reflect upon the grief that idleness brought David the king. When he should have been in battle, he was at home, taking it easy. While idling about his palace he saw a sight that stirred his sexual passions. Still idle, he reflected and meditated upon that experience until it festered into the open sin of covetousness and then adultery. Those sins in turn led to the murder of Uriah, the husband of Bathsheba. Before long the entire affair was public knowledge.

Talk about anxiety! I have no doubt that David at one point would gladly have died rather than lived through the grief and anxiety produced by the harvest of his idleness.

The industry of Paul

Paul the apostle had been pursued by hostility at Berea, and it was necessary for him to flee to Athens—alone! In Athens he could have holed up in some private room and felt sorry for himself. He could have brooded over the mistreatment he had suffered for the work of the Lord. He could have said, "I have been laboring night and day in Thessalonica and preaching faithfully in Berea. Now I will take it easy."

Not Paul. Immediately he began an investigation of conditions in Athens. After acquainting himself with the state of this intellectual metropolis, he began to preach in the synagogue to the Jews and among devout people in the marketplace daily (Acts 17:16-17).

Soon Paul's ministry attracted the interest of the philosophers, the Epicureans and the Stoics. They requested a speech from him in which he would set forth his philosophy. He could have responded, "Oh, no. I was stoned and left for dead at Lystra. I was beaten and jailed in Philippi. I have just now been abused in Berea for this very thing— preaching the gospel of the Son of God, whom I serve."

Paul was not of this stripe, however. Far from feeling sorry for himself, he shared with them the blessed gospel. At their invitation he walked up the stone steps to the top of Areopagus, the ancient heart of Athens from whose crescent of stone seats some judges had 400 years previously condemned Socrates to die. Standing at this place, the ambassador of the Judge of the earth delivered probably the greatest sermon ever to come from the lips of mortal man.

Thorough preparation marked every facet of Paul's ministry. As soon as God had saved him in Damascus, Paul immediately started preparation in Arabia and then in Jerusalem, developing the skill necessary to carry on the work to which God had called him (consider this against the backdrop of the preceding chapter). At Athens, Paul was speaking to the intellectual leaders of the world. The laws of this city pronounced death upon anyone who introduced a foreign deity. Did that stop Paul? He was a Jewish tentmaker whose "bodily presence is weak, and his speech contemptible" (2 Corinthians 10:10)—but he spoke out in that classic and proud city of the ancient world.

It was in the marketplace at Athens that Socrates, the wisest of men, asked his immortal questions. Over in the nearby olive groves by the brook, Plato founded his academy. To the east was the Lyceum of Aristotle. Near at hand in the Agora were the garden of the Epicureans and the painted porch of the Stoics. Here was the home of ancient Greek drama, where scholars spoke with pride the names of Aeschylus and Sophocles. Here the orators of Greece stood up to speak. Here were historians such as Thucydides and Xenophon. In ornate temples the national spirit of Athens was deified in the marble images of their heroes and soldiers, in the trophies of her victories, in her multifarious objects of interest.

Not overawed in this situation, Paul proceeded to teach the Athenians about a God they had never heard of. In the course of his speech he covered a good many topics, including...

- atheism, or the dogma that there is no God
- pantheism, or the belief that everything is God
- materialism, or the notion that the world is eternal
- fatalism, or the superstition that no intelligence presides over the universe, but all things come to pass by necessity or chance
- polytheism, or the fancy that there are many gods
- ritualism, or the imagination that God can be honored by purely external performances
- evolutionism, or the hypothesis that man is a product of natural forces
- optimism, or the delusion that, in this best possible world, man has no sin of which to repent
- unitarianism, or the tenet that Christ was an ordinary man

- annihilationism, or the belief that death is the final end of being

- universalism, or the sentiment that all will be saved

And Paul also expounded the gospel of the one true Savior, Jesus Christ.

Talk about skill! Talk about mastering one's field! Talk about industry both in the preparation and the delivery!

Paul was always engaged in some worthwhile pursuit. Because of his diligence, God was pleased to open up to him doors of opportunity. As a result of Paul's effective execution of his opportunity, God blessed his ministry and at the same time delivered him from fear and anxiety. As Paul himself told the Philippians, "I know both how to be abased, and I know how to abound" (Philippians 4:12).

Paul was so busy he had no time for fear-producing, worry-loaded thoughts. He refused to worry even though he was imprisoned in Rome. Read 2 Timothy 4:13—there, he requests that Timothy bring the "books, but especially the parchments." Again, his mind was on what he could accomplish. Industry! This mighty man of God remained industrious right to the end.

What are you waiting for?

Many people piously assert that they are bound to "wait upon the Lord" and to "trust in the Lord" while they sit on the stool of do-nothing and twiddle their thumbs.

Now it is true that we must wait upon the Lord and trust in Him. Nevertheless, the proof that we are waiting upon the Lord and trusting in Him will be revealed in our "always abounding in the work of the Lord" (1 Corinthians 15:58).

By "abounding in the work" Paul referred to activity with a worthwhile purpose, directed toward a worthwhile goal. This is essential to the poise that conquers worry, because you cannot fasten your mind upon two things at once. You cannot throw all your energies into

God-glorifying activity while at the same time focusing your attention upon fear-producing thoughts.

Consider this: Death is characterized by inaction, life by action. As death approaches, action decreases. It has often been noted, in fact, that decreasing activity hastens death. Do you not know some people who were in good health until their retirement, and then they suddenly fell ill and died? The transition from work to inactivity was too much for them. It was in their nature to work. Deprived of the opportunity to be industrious, they had no further reason to live.

There are some who rationalize their idleness by saying they are advanced in years—that they have worked all their lives and now deserve a rest. Don't think to immunize yourself so naively from the responsibility and benefit of being industrious. Look how many great personalities remained active and productive well into their so-called dotage:

- Golda Meir led the modern nation of Israel in her mid 70s.
- Cornelius Vanderbilt spent most of his life in ferry transport. He built most of his railroads when he was well over 70, making his hundreds of millions at an age when most men have retired.
- The German philosopher Immanuel Kant wrote some of his greatest works when he was past 70.
- Johann Goethe wrote the second part of *Faust* after he was 80.
- Victor Hugo astounded the world with some of his finest writings after his eightieth birthday.
- Alfred Tennyson was 83 when he wrote his poem "Crossing the Bar."
- Viscount Palmerston was prime minister of England at 81, William Gladstone at 83.
- Prince Otto Eduard Leopold von Bismarck was vigorously administering the affairs of the German Empire at 74.

- Francesco Crispi was premier of Italy at 75.

- Verdi wrote operas after he was 80.

- Titian painted his incomparable *Battle of Lepanto* at 98, his *Last Supper* at 99.

- Michelangelo was still sculpting masterpieces at 89.

- Claude Monet was still painting great masterpieces after 85.

More years, more creativity

I believe one of the reasons Sir Winston Churchill and General Douglas MacArthur lived so long was the fact they both knew and utilized the value of industry. People who are busy don't have time for anxiety. Worry is a time thief, and they refuse to be robbed by it.

Norman Cousins, for years the celebrated editor of *Saturday Review*, more than once asserted his belief in a relationship between creativity and longevity. He illustrated his conviction by referring to meetings he had with two men who, when he visited them, were octogenarians—the musician Pablo Casals and the missionary Albert Schweitzer.

He recalls Pablo Casals at eight o'clock in the morning, just before his ninetieth birthday, being assisted by his young wife, Marta, to the piano. Cousins said that watching Casals move made him aware of the man's many infirmities. He had rheumatoid arthritis, emphysema, swollen hands, and clenched fingers. He was badly stooped, and his head pitched over as he shuffled forward.

Then Cousins tells how Casals arranged himself at the piano and began to play the opening bars of Bach's *Well-Tempered Clavier*. It appeared as though a miracle were taking place. Casals's fingers slowly relaxed. His back straightened. He breathed more freely. He hummed as he played. Finally, as he plunged into a Brahms concerto, his fingers, "now agile and powerful, raced across the keyboard with dashing speed."

The older octogenarian, Albert Schweitzer, told Norman Cousins, "I have no intention of dying so long as I can do things. And if I do things, there's no need to die. So I will live a long, long time." Schweitzer lived to 95 years of age.

I concluded a long time ago that people who find joy in their work, and who are committed to a life of productive industry, enjoy the kind of poise conducive to good health and longevity. Furthermore, industry is consistent with God's will for your life and mine.

19

WIN OVER WORRY
by Stewardship

I t's sad but true that many people will put less in the collection plate at church than they will use to buy a ticket for the movies or breakfast at a restaurant. They won't give their money, their time, or their talents. They are afraid of losing out.

Let me be frank with you. No one has a right to expect blessings from God if, through greed and covetousness, he or she blocks the pathway by which God's blessings come. God is the owner of all things. We are stewards. God knew that man would contest this fact and so He went to special pains to make His ownership clear in the opening chapters of the Bible. God's name is mentioned 14 times in the first 13 verses, 31 times in the first chapter, and 45 times in the first two chapters of Genesis.

Stewardship matters not because of God's need, but because of ours. God has no needs: "Every beast of the forest is mine, and the cattle upon a thousand hills...If I were hungry, I would not tell thee: for the world is mine, and the fulness thereof" (Psalm 50:10,12). And again: "The silver is mine, and the gold is mine, saith the LORD of hosts" (Haggai 2:8).

There is a threefold basis for stewardship, according to Isaiah 43:1:

"Now thus saith the Lord that created thee, O Jacob, and he that formed thee, O Israel, Fear not: for I have redeemed thee, I have called thee by thy name; thou art mine." God created us. He redeemed us. And He sustains us. It is impossible for a person to experience the poise that conquers worry unless he possesses an awareness of God's approval.

Without an awareness of divine approval, a person is plagued by feelings of guilt and fear. He may belong to an Amazonian tribe unreached by even the faintest echo of the gospel, but because of that moral monitor God has placed in his breast he will know, deep within, that he is responsible to a higher power. Not until he comes to know this higher power personally through the mediation of Jesus Christ will his guilt be resolved and his fears subside.

Many people are foolishly trying to obtain victory over guilt and fear through a battery of psychoanalytic techniques—Freudian expressionism and catharsis, Gestalt therapy, and the like.

However, only God can banish our fear. Through the instrumentality of the Holy Spirit, He gives us a spirit "of power, and of love, and of a sound mind" (2 Timothy 1:7). Not that we always make use of this privilege. It is possible for a Christian to be out of fellowship with God and thus forfeit the poise that is dependent upon awareness of His approval.

The three principles of God's ownership

God set out three principles in the Bible about the obligations we owe to Him. These transcend the boundaries of time, geography, and race.

1. One day out of seven belongs to God.

This first principle was made clear in the first chapter of the Bible. It has never changed, though it has often been disobeyed and denied and abused. We are still required to honor God by recognizing the day of rest.

2. Substitutionary sacrifice is the only answer to human sin.

This principle also transcends time. Again, we can look back to the early chapters of Genesis. When Abel offered an atoning sacrifice it was in response to this fundamental law and unalterable principle. Hebrews 11:4 tells us that Abel offered his sacrifice "by faith," meaning that there had been a revelation from God concerning it. Now, all sacrifices have had their fulfillment in Christ, "the Lamb of God, which taketh away the sin of the world" (John 1:29).

3. We are called to stewardship of material possessions.

Please pay attention! If you are inclined to get a little impatient with this emphasis on stewardship and turn over to the next chapter, I implore you to hear me out—or rather, to hear God's Word out.

One out of every six verses of the four Gospels has to do with the right and wrong use of material possessions. Sixteen of our Lord's 38 parables have to do with the right and wrong use of material possessions. Don't sin against yourself by ignoring this chapter. Suspend your judgment and "to thine own self be true." Surely more anxiety and insecurity among Christians is caused by deficiency at this point than at any other.

Why is stewardship so important?

In the Garden of Eden, God kept to Himself the tree of the knowledge of good and evil. This He did to remind Adam and Eve of their duty of stewardship and of God's right of ownership. They were not to touch the fruit of that tree. In a special sense, it belonged to God. True, everything belongs to God, but a certain proportion of that which He bestows upon us is to be set aside immediately and with no strings attached.

Is it not traditional that the tenant farmer in the Midwest be required to give back to the owner one-fourth of the corn crop? Is it not traditional that the tenant farmer in the South be required to give back to the landowner one-third of the cotton crop? Because God is the owner of all things, is it not fair that we be required to give back to Him a proportion of that which He makes possible?

Philippians 4:5 says, "Let your moderation be known unto all men. The Lord is at hand." The word "moderation" means "fairness," among other things. There is no poise without fairness, and there is no fairness without stewardship of material possessions. This poise that brings peace is significantly dependent upon our obedience to stewardship opportunities.

Some folks think giving is meant to finance the local church, as though it were a tax. But to think this is to miss the whole point. We don't give out of duty. We give from an inner compulsion, returning to God through the tithe, and offerings above the tithe, as the Lord prospers us.

We practice stewardship for three reasons:

1. In recognition of God's sovereign ownership.

"Thou shalt remember the LORD thy God: for it is he that giveth thee power to get wealth, that he may establish his covenant which he sware unto thy fathers, as it is this day" (Deuteronomy 8:18). Paul picked up the same point in the New Testament: "What? know ye not that your body is the temple of the Holy Ghost which is in you, which ye have of God, and ye are not your own? For ye are bought with a price: therefore glorify God in your body, and in your spirit, which are God's" (1 Corinthians 6:19-20).

2. In appreciative acknowledgment of redeeming grace.

"By grace are ye saved through faith; and that not of yourselves: it is the gift of God: not of works, lest any man should boast. For we are his workmanship, created in Christ Jesus unto good works, which God hath before ordained that we should walk in them" (Ephesians 2:8-10).

3. In surrender of life and talents to the Lord.

"I beseech you therefore, brethren, by the mercies of God, that ye present your bodies a living sacrifice, holy, acceptable unto God, which is your reasonable service. And be not conformed to this world: but be ye transformed by the renewing of your mind, that ye may prove what is that good, and acceptable, and perfect, will of God" (Romans 12:1-2).

When you prepare your tithe, you prepare for worship. When you put your money in the collection plate, you are saying, in essence, "This is a tangible expression of my total surrender to Thee. This money that I place in this plate represents my brains, my blood, my abilities— all of the blessings that have come from Thee, for I realize that 'every good gift and every perfect gift is from above, and cometh down from the Father of lights, with whom is no variableness, neither shadow of turning' (James 1:17). It is because of the health, because of the mental ability, because of the friends, because of the various resources that Thou hast given me that I am able to make a living. All that I am and all that I have is Thine. My stewardship of material possessions is but an expression of that fact."

The truth about tithing

The basis of our monetary responsibility is the tithe. Tithing is paying back to God ten percent of the increase. And God doesn't mince His words concerning those who fail to obey. The Bible says that if you fail to pay that ten percent back into the "storehouse" (Malachi 3:10) with faithful regularity you are a thief and a robber.

There are those who argue that the responsibility of tithing was in force only during the days of the law—from the time of Moses to the time of Christ. They will tell you that Malachi 3:10 has no relevance for today because it is in the Old Testament.

The Lord must have known that such mischief would arise. Therefore He introduced the words of Malachi 3:6, "For I am the LORD, I change not..." After these words He called Israel back to His ordinances, to tithes and offerings, to the storehouse, and to His conditional promise of blessing. The New Testament reaffirms these words of Malachi

3:6 by saying that with God there is "no variableness, neither shadow of turning" (James 1:17).

The same people who say that tithing was for those under the law will, of course, turn in the next moment to Psalm 23 for comfort, to Psalm 32 for guidance, to Job for wisdom, and to Elijah for a pattern of prayer—among many other Old Testament passages. To be consistent, these people who throw out Malachi 3:10 ought also to throw out John 3:16. After all, this too was spoken prior to the time that redemption was completed by our Lord on the cross of Calvary.

In fact, tithing was not a product of the law. Tithing antedated the law. Abraham tithed. The law of the tithe is not an Israelite law. It is a fundamental and unalterable law of God. It is still in force. That is why tithing is commended by Jesus. "Woe unto you, scribes and Pharisees, hypocrites! For ye pay tithe of mint and anise and cummin, and have omitted the weightier matters of the law, judgment, mercy, and faith: these ought ye to have done, and not to leave the other undone" (Matthew 23:23).

Just as Abraham paid tithes to Melchizedek, so we pay tithes to Christ. In Hebrews 7 this truth is made clear. The Son of God who lives and abides as a priest continually after the order of Melchizedek "receiveth tithes" (verse 8)—that is, receives them now!

When paying tithes, Abraham acknowledged Melchizedek's sovereignty as a king-priest. Likewise, today when paying tithes, we acknowledge Christ as Sovereign and Lord. Refusal to pay the tithe is refusal to own Christ as Sovereign and High Priest. Thus one makes Christ not only inferior to Melchizedek, but also inferior to the Levites, the priestly group of Old Testament times.

The tithe was incorporated in the law because it was a principle worthy of divine enforcement. God never repealed the fundamental law of tithing; grace has not annulled it; time has not altered it. For that reason, Malachi's command concerning the tithe retains all its original force:

Will a man rob God? Yet ye have robbed me. But ye say,
Wherein have we robbed thee? In tithes and offerings. Ye
are cursed with a curse: for ye have robbed me, even this
whole nation. Bring ye all the tithes into the storehouse,
that there may be meat in mine house, and prove me now
herewith, saith the LORD of hosts, if I will not open you the
windows of heaven, and pour you out a blessing, that there
shall not be room enough to receive it. And I will rebuke
the devourer for your sakes, and he shall not destroy the
fruits of your ground; neither shall your vine cast her fruit
before the time in the field, saith the LORD of hosts. And
all nations shall call you blessed: for ye shall be a delight-
some land, saith the LORD of hosts (Malachi 3:8-12).

In this command, Malachi makes the practice of tithing a condition for receiving God's blessing in a special way and to a special
degree. The implication is clear. When we refuse to tithe we are rob-
bing God, we make ourselves subject to a curse, and we deny ourselves
the blessings of God.

Tithing didn't disappear in the New Testament

Grace does not abrogate the law. Grace fulfills the law and goes
much further than the most stringent demands of the law. Grace provides the dynamic necessary for fulfilling the law's mechanics. The
law told man what to do, but failed to provide him with the capabil-
ity to accomplish it. Grace provides the dynamic of the Holy Spirit
whereby in the strength of God we fulfill the demands of the law,
and much more.

Jesus said,

Think not that I am come to destroy the law, or the prophets: I am not come to destroy, but to fulfill. For verily I
say unto you, Till heaven and earth pass, one jot or one
tittle shall in no wise pass from the law, till all be fulfilled.

Whosoever therefore shall break one of these least commandments, and shall teach men so, he shall be called the
least in the kingdom of heaven: but whosoever shall do and
teach them, the same shall be called great in the kingdom of
heaven. For I say unto you, That except your righteousness
shall exceed the righteousness of the scribes and Pharisees,
ye shall in no case enter into the kingdom of heaven (Matthew 5:17-20).

We have already seen how Jesus commended the tithing of the
Pharisees. In verse 20 of Matthew 5, the Lord tells us that our righteousness must exceed the righteousness of the scribes and Pharisees.
Grace fulfills and amplifies the law, instead of destroying and mini-
mizing it.

Proceed further in Matthew 5. The law says, "Thou shalt not kill"
(verse 21). Jesus makes it clear that if a man hates his brother he is just
as guilty as if he had murdered him. The law says, "Thou shalt not
commit adultery" (verse 27). Jesus points out that under grace whosoever looks on a woman to lust after her has already violated the seventh commandment in his heart.

Carry this principle over in the matter of the stewardship of money.
How can an enlightened child of God do less under grace than the
Jew did under the law? The Jew gave offerings over and above his tithe,
too. For instance, if you study the Old Testament, you will discover
that the Temple and its furnishings were paid for by offerings over
and above the tithes.

There is always a question mark in my mind about the person
who goes to extremes to prove that we are under no obligation to
tithe. What is his motive? In Leviticus 27:30 God makes it clear that
"The tithe…is the LORD's." Therefore we, as stewards, have absolutely no right to handle it as though it were ours. It must be placed
where God says and when God says—namely, in the storehouse on
the Lord's day.

The money belongs to God

Jesus said, "Render therefore unto Caesar the things which are Caesar's; and unto God the things that are God's" (Matthew 22:21). In other words, pay your taxes and pay your tithes. Your taxes belong to the government. The proof of this lies in the fact that they are deducted from your pay before you receive it. Your United States income tax is to be paid to the collector at the Internal Revenue Service at a given location.

Suppose you, an American, owed the government an income tax of $1,000. Suppose that you made out your tax form and attached a note to it in which you said:

> Dear Uncle Sam,
>
> You will notice that I owe you $1,000. I am sending $100 to my local postmaster. He is one of your faithful servants and he is having a hard time financially. I am sending $100 to a U.S.O. down in South Carolina. They are doing a magnificent work boosting the morale of your own servicemen, and they need help desperately. I am sending $100 to a nephew of mine who is a sailor with the Seventh Fleet. He is liable to get blown up any time and I think that he needs encouragement. After all, he is one of your faithful servicemen. Then I am sending $200 to the Veterans Administration. After all, they are loyally dedicated to carrying out your will. But, Uncle Sam, just to let you know my heart is in the right place, I am sending the remaining $500 to the collector at the Internal Revenue Service in my area here.

It's absurd. Why? Because the law of the country does not extend to you the right to decide how the tax money should be distributed. It doesn't belong to you. Therefore, your only responsibility is to hand it over.

Imagine a man who owes God a tithe of $1,000. But instead of accepting God's revelation that "the tithe...is the LORD's," he says, "The tithe is mine. It's my tithe!" Then, acting on that premise, he high-handedly determines the distribution of the money that is not his in the first place. He sends $100 to a radio evangelist, another $100 to a Bible school, and another $100 to a missionary.

That is not what God requires. The tithe is to go into the "storehouse," which, in this age, is the church. Hear the Word of the Lord:

> Upon the first day of the week let every one of you lay by him in store, as God hath prospered him, that there be no gatherings when I come (1 Corinthians 16:2).

> Bring ye all the tithes into the storehouse, that there may be meat in mine house, and prove me now herewith, saith the LORD of hosts, if I will not open you the windows of heaven, and pour you out a blessing, that there shall not be room enough to receive it (Malachi 3:10).

The word that is translated "store" in 1 Corinthians 16:2 is the same word that was used in the Greek Septuagint to translate "storehouse" in Malachi 3:10. In other words, it would be a correct translation of 1 Corinthians 16:2 to say, "Upon the first day of the week let every one of you lay by him in the storehouse..."

Who should receive the tithe?

Now I should add here that these scriptural truths are set out here by one who doesn't pastor a local church. Rather, I lead a parachurch organization dependent upon the gifts of God's people made above their tithes. Gifts over and above one's tithes can be made to Christian causes. But "the tithe...is the LORD's." The specific depository is the local church, and it is to be placed there undesignated.

In 1957, when the Lord led me to resign the pastorate to go into the field of evangelism, a dear friend who fought this truth said, "Haggai, now I reckon you will abandon this foolishness about storehouse tithing."

"My change in ministry doesn't mean a change in Scripture or commitment," I replied.

"Follow that notion, and in a year you will collapse for lack of support," he insisted.

Said I, "If this ministry is of God, He'll supply the need."

It was, and He has.

When a man refuses to tithe his money, he is repeating, in kind, if not in degree, the sin of Adam and Eve. In partaking of the forbidden fruit, they took to themselves an authority that was not theirs. That tree belonged to God, not to them. When we do not tithe, we are taking to ourselves an authority that is not ours. We are appropriating money that belongs to God. How, then, can we expect peace? How can we expect victory over anxiety and freedom from worry? For God, and God alone, is the Author of peace.

Going back to the man who will not honor God by paying the tithe—what will he do when his little child becomes critically ill and doctors say there is no hope apart from supernatural intervention? That same man will fall on his face before God and say, "O God, this is my child, bone of my bones, flesh of my flesh, blood of my blood. I hand him to Thee. Do what seems good in Thy sight. If it can please Thee, restore him to health and strength and to us."

Such hypocrisy! He is willing to trust God with his own flesh and blood, yet he will not trust God with his silver and gold. Does he think more of his money than he does of his child? How can God honor a man like that? How can God justly bless a man who turns his back upon God as soon as it suits him—turns his back upon God by refusing to tithe?

Here's another illustration: In Mark 12:41-44, Jesus was watching some people as they cast money into the treasury. Some put in a lot of money. By contrast, a poor widow put in two mites—everything she had. Jesus called His disciples together and said, "This poor widow hath cast more in, than all they which have cast into the treasury" (verse 43).

How could Jesus know? Perhaps they had put part of their tithe into a religious foundation, or some Bible college, or sent it to some radio evangelist. You say, "They didn't have such things back then!"

That's true, but it is a fact of history that there were more depositories for the giving of alms in that day than there are today. The others at the treasury could have said they had given much of their tithe to charitable causes. Jesus judged their stewardship on the basis of what they put into the treasury of the house of God, which today is our literal, visible, local church.

Consider the process of bringing the tithe:

First, you bring the tithe in *physically*. This links tithing with worship. The two are inseparable.

Second, you bring *all* the tithe. You don't deduct your doctor's bills, your transportation to and from work, your insurance policies, your gifts to the Red Cross, United Way, and so forth. You bring a full ten percent of your total increase.

Third, you bring all the tithe *into the storehouse*. When this is done, your responsibility ceases. Even when Paul was trying to get money together for the church in Jerusalem, he didn't tell the Corinthian Christians to send their tithe there. He told them to put their tithe in their local church. Only then did he urge the church to help out its sister congregation in Jerusalem.

You get back what you give out—and more

Now notice the conditional promise of Malachi 3:10: "Prove me now herewith, saith the Lord of hosts, if I will not open you the windows of heaven, and pour you out a blessing, that there shall not be room enough to receive it."

If I could not believe what God says about tithing, I could not believe what He says about anything. It is strange that people will believe what He says about salvation, what He says about heaven, what He says about hell, what He says about baptism, and what He says about soul-winning, yet they will not believe what He says about tithing and the stewardship of possessions.

I know a wealthy man who has set up a religious foundation. He allegedly puts ten percent of his earnings into that foundation and therefore considers himself a tither. However, he does not put the tithe where God says to put it. In addition to that manifest disobedience, one of his corporations borrows the money that is in the nonprofit religious foundation, and does so on highly preferential terms. Therefore he has access to money on which he doesn't need to pay a tax—money that he uses to expand his business.

You say, "Well, God is blessing him." Is He? The trouble is that too many people think only in terms of money when they think of God opening the windows of heaven and pouring out blessings.

I know another man who recently made $40 million in a single year, but because of an ulcerated stomach he can't eat a decent piece of meat. There are some men who would give all of their money if they could buy peace of mind, the respect of their children, and the love of their wife.

Once again, let me remind you that from a selfish standpoint it would be to my advantage to preach that a person has a right to place his tithe where he wants, inasmuch as on that basis additional money could be secured to finance my own nonprofit organization. But I know that God would not bless it.

Some time ago a dear friend of mine suggested that a group of businessmen give $10,000 a year out of their tithes to support the ministry God has given me. I thanked him for his generous proposal but said quite frankly, "You are barking up a tree where was never found a possum. I would no more be party to accepting a part of your tithe—a tithe which is not yours, but God's—than I would be party to taking a portion of your income tax, which is not yours, but Uncle Sam's."

You say, "What does this have to do with worry?"

Plenty! If you went downtown and stole $100 from a merchant, would you have peace of mind? No. You would probably think that people were talking about you every time they looked at you. You would feel uncomfortable whenever you were in the vicinity of the business you had stolen from and to which you are now indebted.

In the fourth chapter of Philippians, from which the textual basis of our formula for victory over worry is found, Paul commends the monetary liberality of the Philippians. Is it not interesting that the Philippian church was the only church in which Paul found no doctrinal or ethical error?

Many people glibly quote Philippians 4:19: "My God shall supply all your need according to his riches in glory by Christ Jesus." But may I suggest that the fulfillment of that promise is conditional upon a spirit akin to that expressed by the Philippians, and recorded in the immediately preceding verses?

One of the reasons many people worry is financial adversity—an adversity sometimes begotten of their own disobedience in the area of stewardship. "Honor the Lord with thy substance, and with the firstfruits of all thine increase: So shall thy barns be filled with plenty, and thy presses shall burst out with new wine" (Proverbs 3:9-10). Those words were written under the inspiration of the Holy Spirit of God.

Failure to tithe is incontrovertible evidence that you are more interested in yourself than you are in the work of the Lord. One of the chief causes of anxiety and worry is self-centeredness. "Where your treasure is, there will your heart be also" (Matthew 6:21).

When your chief concern is not merely how to tithe, but how to give offerings—generous offerings over and above the tithe given to the glory of God—you will experience a joy and a peace the world cannot define. But when you refuse to tithe, you do so either from ignorance or covetousness, and God's Word states that covetousness is idolatry: "Mortify therefore your members which are upon the earth; fornication, uncleanness, inordinate affection, evil concupiscence, and covetousness, which is idolatry" (Colossians 3:5).

Money so easily becomes a tin god. We resemble our gods; we

assimilate what we conceive to be desirable. When money is your god there is no peace. But if Christ is the Lord of your life—the dominant dynamic of your experience, the overmastering passion of your interests—then you inevitably begin to resemble Him who "is our peace" (Ephesians 2:14). As a result of your fellowship with Him, you will experience the peace only He can give. "Peace I leave with you, my peace I give unto you: not as the world giveth, give I unto you. Let not your heart be troubled, neither let it be afraid" (John 14:27).

Open yourself to the blessings that God promises to those who honor Him with their substance.

20

WIN OVER WORRY
by Surrender

After hearing a missionary who had returned from China, a young lady walked up to her and said, "I'd give the world to have your experience."

"That," said the missionary, "is exactly what it cost me."

I am impressed time after time when I listen to missionaries on furlough from a foreign field. They have willingly forfeited economic affluence, worldly ease, and the fellowship of relatives and friends here at home. They have a serenity, a poise that bespeaks a peace that cannot be defined—"the peace of God, which passeth all understanding" (Philippians 4:7).

The Word of God commends this kind of surrender—and not just for missionaries:

> Neither yield ye your members as instruments of unrighteousness unto sin: but yield yourselves unto God, as those that are alive from the dead, and your members as instruments of righteousness unto God (Romans 6:13).

> What things were gain to me, those I counted loss for Christ. Yea doubtless, and I count all things but loss for the excellency

of the knowledge of Christ Jesus my Lord: for whom I have suffered the loss of all things, and do count them but dung, that I may win Christ (Philippians 3:7-8).

He that findeth his life shall lose it: and he that loseth his life for my sake shall find it (Matthew 10:39).

To be sure, the person who has totally surrendered himself to Christ fulfills all the other contributory factors to poise that have already been mentioned. All these aspects interlink and overlap; they are arranged like the facets of a diamond. I have been turning the jewel of poise around and around so that it may be viewed from every angle and that light may be flashed from every side of it.

There's less hassle on the narrow path

Many times while in the pastorate, and even on occasions since entering the field of evangelism, I have been approached by people who said, in substance, "I know that if I yield my life to the Lord He is going to make me preach, and I don't want to do it."

With some it wasn't preaching, but some other sphere of service. There are people who apparently are plagued with the misconception that if they surrender themselves to the Lord He will require of them that which they do not want to do.

This is a trick of the devil. When you surrender yourself to the Lord you will want what the Lord wants for you. God's Word says, "Delight thyself also in the LORD; and he shall give thee the desires of thine heart" (Psalm 37:4). And, "If ye abide in me, and my words abide in you, ye shall ask what ye will, and it shall be done unto you" (John 15:7).

God's Word tells us that if we, as human parents, give good gifts to our children, how much more will our heavenly Father give good things unto them who ask Him (see Matthew 7:11). Imagine your son or daughter coming to you and saying, "Mom and Dad, I want to do everything that will make you happy. I know that you have much more experience than I, and there are many mistakes that I can avoid by following your counsel and advice. I beg of you to guide me and direct me. To the best of my ability I will follow your suggestions."

Can you imagine, in response, retreating into a private room with your wife or husband and plotting together, saying, "Now little Jimmy has put himself completely in our hands. He is at our mercy. Therefore, let us do everything we can to make him as awkward and miserable and frustrated as possible"?

That's absurd. If we would not treat our own children that way, how much more true is it that our heavenly Father would not treat us that way? "If ye then, being evil, know how to give good gifts unto your children, how much more shall your Father which is in heaven give good things to them that ask him?" (Matthew 7:11). "Like as a father pitieth his children, so the LORD pitieth them that fear him" (Psalm 103:13).

With surrender comes poise that conquers worry. Lot pitched his tent toward Sodom. Too bad. Lot was a child of God—2 Peter 2:7-8 makes that clear. But Lot went his way instead of God's way. As a result of his disobedience he lost—and lost dearly. The Lord told him to get out of Sodom. His married daughters, his sons-in-law, and his grandchildren would not leave with him. Parents may take their children to Sodom, but rarely will they get their children out again once they have been there any length of time.

Lot lost his wife. She was turned into a pillar of salt. He lost all his possessions, his position in the city, his prestige. He lost the respect of his two married daughters, who, in a cave, got him drunk and then committed incest with him, whereby he became the father of one son by each of them.

The grief and anxiety that would have been spared him had Lot only surrendered himself to the Lord! He was robbed of the "desires of his heart" because he refused to "delight himself in the Lord."

Surrender begins with a single step

A young mother asked to see me during a series of speaking engagements in a distant city. I told her I did not do counseling. Her pastor, a senior man of godly discernment, pled with me to break my rule and see this lady. I agreed.

She was greatly distraught, mentally and emotionally. The anguish of her heart was torturing her body and imprinting her face. She had been under psychiatric care for more than four-and-a-half years, during which time she had been subjected to shock treatments. She, a professing Christian, gave every evidence of sincerely wanting to do the will of God.

After some brief but pertinent questioning, I asked her frankly if there was something that had taken place in her life, whether years ago or more recently, that preyed constantly on her mind.

She said there was. It was a sin committed during adolescence. I asked her if she had confessed it to the Lord. She assured me that she had. Since a second person had been involved, and a third knew about it, the thought that her dereliction might surface terrified her. She couldn't stand the prospect that her children, now entering their teens, might find out. She seriously considered suicide.

I said, "I imagine, from my observation, that you have confessed it to the Lord over and over and over—probably a thousand times. Is that right?"

She nodded her head affirmatively.

I said, "You see, actually, you are making God a liar. You confessed that sin once. God promised you absolute forgiveness, as we read in the words of 1 John 1:9: 'If we confess our sins, he is faithful and just to forgive us our sins, and to cleanse us from all unrighteousness.'"

I added, "The reason you are going through this torture arises from your unwillingness to surrender yourself completely to the Lord. You do not trust Him. You are not willing to take Him at His Word. He has forgiven you, but you refuse to believe it. You refuse to forgive yourself. You are making the mistake of thinking that repentance is repining, and that self-examination is brooding. Now then, simply take God at His Word.

"Surrender your life completely to Him. Surrender the limitations of your finite mind to the assurance of His unchangeable Word. He has forgiven you. Now in complete surrender, believe it. I can't promise the truth will never surface, or that your children will never learn of it. But, by your current brooding, almost psychotic brooding, you are now depriving your children of the mother they need. And, remember the promise of our Lord: 'My grace is sufficient for thee: for My strength is made perfect in weakness'" (2 Corinthians 12:9).

Her husband later said, "I don't know what has happened to her, but she is a different woman. She has a sparkle and a vibrancy I have never seen in her before. Even the children remark about it."

Businessmen across the world, petrified by fear and paralyzed by anxiety over reverses in their business, could enjoy business success and more if they would only surrender themselves to God and take Him as their partner.

Homes, internally divorced, where husband and wife live together under protest in an atmosphere of tension, could become the vestibule of heaven if husband and wife would simply surrender to Jesus Christ. It is trite, but it is nevertheless true that if their home were built upon the Rock, Christ Jesus, it would not be headed for the rocks of chaos. Here, then, is the secret of poise: surrender to Christ.

Remember: "I can do all things through Christ which strengtheneth me" (Philippians 4:13). He will strengthen you to observe the laws of self-control, relaxation, scheduling, stewardship, skill, industry, thought control, and enthusiasm—all the contributory factors in the mastery of poise—if you will only surrender your will to Him.

21

WIN OVER WORRY
by Prayer

Prayer is the best cell phone you will ever have. You can use it anywhere (even in the subway) and it connects you to the Creator of the universe. It is direct and personal.

Paul's formula for victory over worry is praise, poise, and prayer. You cannot omit prayer. That is why Paul's answer goes so far beyond positive thinking. To win over worry, you must effectively connect with God. As Paul said, "Be careful for nothing; but in every thing by prayer and supplication with thanksgiving let your requests be made known unto God" (Philippians 4:6).

Peace is possible only to those who have related themselves to God through Christ, who is the Prince of Peace. The Bible declares, "There is no peace, saith my God, to the wicked" (Isaiah 57:21). By "the wicked" is meant not only the guttersnipes, the ne'er-do-wells, the riffraff of society. The wicked are those who, unrepentant of their sins, have either refused or neglected to come to the Son of God by faith. They have not received Him into their hearts.

Prayer takes us to the heart of life

Read very carefully, for what you are about to read is a staggering truth:

> You hath he quickened, who were dead in trespasses and
> sins wherein in time past ye walked according to the course
> of this world, according to the prince of the power of the
> air, the spirit that now worketh in the children of disobe-
> dience (Ephesians 2:1-2).

God's Word here states that until you receive Jesus Christ as your Savior and Lord, you are "dead in trespasses and sins." As one who is dead in trespasses and sins, you are dead to God and to every quality inherent in His nature.

What are these qualities? Among them are holiness, righteousness, love, truth, wisdom, justice, and power. If you are dead to God, you are therefore dead and insensitive to holiness, righteousness, love, truth, wisdom, justice, and power.

Now pause just a moment and think about what that means. To be sure, those who are dead in sin and therefore dead to God have set up standards. Unfortunately they are not God's standards. "Every man is a law unto himself." That explains marital discord, domestic strife, civil factiousness, labor-management antagonism, national crime, and international tensions.

A person dead in sin and therefore dead to God is alive to Satan and to the qualities inherent in his nature. Some of these qualities are sin, hostility, error, folly, injustice, weakness, and fear. A child of disobedience is dominated and controlled by Satan. Read Ephesians 2:1-2 again: Satan is "the spirit that now worketh in the children of disobedience."

Someone might object, "Well, I'm not a drunkard. I'm not a murderer. I'm not sexually promiscuous. I don't steal or blaspheme."

Of course not. It is not in Satan's interests that everyone take sin to extremes. He transforms himself as an angel of philosophic light, moral light, social light, political light, and cultural light. Satan is a master of public relations.

Until you come to Jesus Christ as a self-confessed sinner and by faith accept the salvation that He has provided, you are spiritually dead. Death means separation. Physical death means separation of the body from the personality. By personality I refer to all of the unseen facets of our being, including soul, spirit, mind, and heart. Spiritual death is our separation in this life from God. Eternal death is our irremediable and unalterable separation from God forever.

Now, if you are spiritually dead, you are separated from God. Therefore you have no peace. Nor can you have any peace. You can use the power of positive thinking, resort to Gestalt psychology, or adhere to Freudian therapy, but it all will be to no avail. Your only hope is in Christ, the Prince of Peace, through whom you have access to God.

Life is union, just as death is separation. Physical life is the union of the body and the personality. Spiritual life is union with God through Christ. When you receive the Lord Jesus Christ as your Savior, you do not merely receive a new concept, a new creed, or a new formula for living. You receive a Person—"Christ in you" (Colossians 1:27). You receive a new nature: "Whereby are given unto us exceeding great and precious promises: that by these ye might be partakers of the divine nature, having escaped the corruption that is in the world through lust" (2 Peter 1:4).

Eternal life is the life of God in the soul of the believer. For the child of God, that which we call physical death is but a transition from life to life more abundant, from time to eternity, from the finite into the infinite. Therefore when one receives spiritual life, he receives in kind, though not in degree, right here and now, everything that he will enjoy in heaven: communion with God, the favor of God, victory over sin, a transcendent love, divine motivation, and peace.

As mentioned, the formula for peace—victory over worry—is praise, poise, and prayer. No unbeliever can have this perfect peace. The prayer of the unrighteous is an abomination before God (see Proverbs 28:9). God will not hear those who persist in unbelief. "If I regard iniquity in my heart, the Lord will not hear me" (Psalm 66:18).

The only way anyone can come to God is through Jesus Christ. "Jesus saith unto him, I am the way, the truth, and the life: no man cometh unto the Father, but by me" (John 14:6). The blind man whom Christ healed in John 9 stated the truth—a truth that is refuted nowhere in God's Word—when he said, "Now we know that God heareth not sinners: but if any man be a worshipper of God, and doeth his will, him he heareth" (John 9:31).

Three Greek words for prayer

What are the detailed practicalities about prayer? Paul gives us this instruction:

> Be careful for nothing; but in every thing by prayer and supplication with thanksgiving let your requests be made known unto God (Philippians 4:6).

Paul uses three different Greek words for prayer in this verse:

- The first word, translated "prayer," refers to a general offering up of wishes and desires to God. This word points to the frame of mind required in the petitioner—a mind of devotion. The word refers to unrestricted concourse between human beings and God. That which brings greatest glory to God, and profit to you, is the habit of prayer. We might call it the Prayer Mood or the Prayer Disposition. It includes adoration, thanksgiving, confession, and intercession.

- The second word, translated "supplication," comes from a Greek word meaning "entreaty," a "seeking," "need," "indigence." It refers to an entreaty impelled by a great sense of need, an extreme want. In fact, the verb form of this word in the original Greek text means "to want." Therefore this word refers distinctly to the petitionary prayers that are expressive of personal need. This prayer is a special petition for the supply of wants, an act of solicitation. It refers strictly to an entreaty to God to supply our needs and wants.

• The third word, translated "requests," refers to those things a Christian asks—even demands—of God.

Nothing is off-limits for prayer

One day my father was replacing a burned-out bulb in the taillight of our old car. While replacing the lens he noticed he had lost a little screw in the tall grass. He had an urgent appointment that night and not much time to spare. He searched and searched for the little screw, but to no avail.

My younger brother, Tom, then five or six years old, was playing next door with a friend. Finally Dad called him and his friend over to help find the screw. When Dad told them what he wanted, Tom asked, "Have you prayed about it?"

My father replied, "No, I haven't, Tom." Tom said, "Well let's pray, Daddy."

Tom then prayed along the following lines: "Heavenly Father, Daddy has lost the screw that he needs for the car. He can't find it and he needs it badly. Help us to find it. Thank You, Jesus. Amen."

Believe it or not, as soon as Tom had finished his prayer, Dad put his hand down in the grass and retrieved the screw. Coincidence? Not at all! It was a distinct answer to prayer.

Because you worry about everything, pray about everything. As Paul said in Philippians 4:6, "In every thing by prayer and supplication with thanksgiving let your requests be made known unto God."

You may pray about the smallest thing or the greatest thing. Set no boundaries with respect to God's care. It is a wide-open field. You may pray for the fullness of the Holy Spirit. You may also pray for a new pair of shoes. Pray to God about the food you eat, the water you drink, the clothing you wear.

Does God not attend to the funeral of every sparrow? Has He not numbered the hairs on our heads? (Matthew 10:29-31). Even the things you think of as big are a small matter to him—though He treats them as important. Our entire earth is like a speck of sand on the beach in comparison to the size of the universe. If you worry about the smallest things, pray about the smallest things.

Peter said to pray "casting all your care upon him; for he careth for you" (1 Peter 5:7). The words translated "care" here are two distinctly different words in the Greek text. The first is the same term translated elsewhere as "anxiety," which we discussed earlier with reference to worry and the divided mind. The other refers to God's solicitous interest in our highest good. The verse, then, invites us to throw all our mind-dividing worries onto Him, for He is desirous of the best for us. Throw all your worries down.

There is an old song by Charles Albert Tindley in which the chorus says:

> Leave it there, leave it there.
> Take your burden to the Lord
>   and leave it there.
> If you trust and never doubt,
> He will surely bring you out.
> Take your burden to the Lord
>   and leave it there.

How to leave your burden

The trouble is, we pretend to take our burdens to the Lord, but instead of leaving them with Him, we take them all home again.

Close friends of our family lived in Darlington, Maryland, in the early 1940s. The husband and father was a classmate of my father during their school days. This Darlington couple had eight children.

The mother, whom we affectionately called Aunt Edith, was coming home from a neighbor's house one Saturday afternoon. As she came nearer to the house she saw her five youngest children huddled together and preoccupied with something of great interest. After some minutes of trying to discover the center of the attraction, she came close enough to see they were playing with baby skunks!

Aghast, she cried at the top of her voice, "Children, run!" At which point each child picked up a skunk and ran!

Isn't that exactly what we do with our burdens and cares? We take them to the Lord in prayer, and He says, "Leave them and run!" Instead, we hug them so close that the smell of them clings to us and we wonder why our friends find our presence nauseating! Yet no problem we have as a Christian is too great or too small for God to deal with. Leave the problem with Him. That is a thrilling thought that you would do well to ponder.

A.T. Pierson, a Bible teacher, sat one day with George Müller, the founder of many English orphanages. Müller was relating to Pierson some of the marvelous things God had done for the orphanage he founded in Bristol. As Müller talked he wrote, and by and by Pierson noticed that he was having difficulty with his pen point. Suddenly Müller bowed his head for a moment in prayer, and then began writing again. Pierson asked what he had prayed about.

"This pen point," replied Müller. "It's not working properly. This is an important letter, and I was asking the Lord to help me so I could write clearly."

"Dear me," replied Pierson. "A man who trusts God for millions of pounds also prays about a scratchy pen point!"

If George Müller had been like many of us, he would have become hot and bothered about his malfunctioning pen. Possibly he would have gotten exasperated with the man who sold him the pen or the company that made it. Perhaps he would have indulged in a little morbid reflection as to why he didn't buy a pen of another make instead of this miserable instrument that was causing him so much trouble. Or he might have thrown the pen down in disgust and given up on the letter, with the result that his conscience would have needled him later for not having written it.

In all kinds of ways, stress and anxiety could have been multiplied by this tiny incident. But they weren't, because George Müller wasn't afraid to pray over a small matter like a scratchy pen.

Anything big enough to worry about is big enough to pray about

This book talks about a formula for winning over worry. But that formula will not work unless you enlist the power of almighty God. In your prayer ask God for the grace to enable you to rejoice, to control your feelings, to count your blessings. Ask Him for the grace to respond to ingratitude with serenity. Call upon Him for the grace of becoming genuinely interested in other people. By prayer, call upon God to help you live in the consciousness of His nearness and therefore to display that poise that is the hallmark of God's presence within you. Ask God to give you the grace to "gird up the loins of your mind" so that you might have the mind of Christ. "Let this mind be in you, which was also in Christ Jesus" (Philippians 2:5).

Through prayer you will enlist divine help in the matters of self-control, relaxation, enthusiasm, scheduling, living each day to the fullest, developing skills, and being industrious. Through prayer, spend time with God until you know His mind and do His will in the all-important matter of stewardship. Through the right kind of prayer life, you will be strengthened to live the surrendered life so essential to the poise that conquers worry.

Through prayer you can duplicate the request of earnest men and women many years ago, who, turning to Jesus, said, "Teach us to pray." The direct answers of God in response to your prayer will give you the strength to battle and conquer the vicious sin of worry. Apart from the blessings of prayer itself there is also a therapeutic value in the actual time spent in quiet before God.

Pray about everything. Pray, and win over worry.

22

WIN OVER WORRY
by Weakness

Prayer is the means whereby we make contact with God's strength. Only when we set aside our own strength will we find ourselves supported.

The Lord Himself is our strength. Don't pray, "Lord, give me strength" as though you are asking Him for a quality distinct from Himself. Rather say, "O Lord, be Thou my strength." The apostle Paul made the source of our strength clear in Ephesians 3:20: "Now unto him that is able to do exceeding abundantly above all that we ask or think, according to the power that worketh in us." The word translated "worketh" is from the Greek word *energeo.* And the word translated "power" is the Greek word *dunamis,* from which we get the word dynamic.

Just as Satan and his powers of darkness energize the unbeliever, so God energizes the obedient Christian. He becomes the divine dynamic whereby the believer conquers all things, including worry. The same power that burnishes each star, points each blade of grass, hurls each wave upon the shore, formed the body of our Savior, raised Jesus from the dead, and will raise our bodies or transfigure them in the hour of glory is the same power that is available to each obedient Christian. This power is made available through prayer.

But remember: This power is available only to those who are weak.

God's helpfulness is meted out only to those who confess their helplessness. "He said unto me, My grace is sufficient for thee: for my strength is made perfect in weakness. Most gladly therefore will I rather glory in my infirmities, that the power of Christ may rest upon me. Therefore I take pleasure in infirmities, in reproaches, in necessities, in persecutions, in distresses for Christ's sake: for when I am weak, then am I strong" (2 Corinthians 12:9-10).

Our strength lies in childlike helplessness. In your helplessness through prayer, cast yourself upon Him who is our strength. The very essence of the meaning of prayer is that you need help beyond your own strength.

The reason many of us do not pray is that we are too strong—strong in our own false, swaggering, blustering strength. We are strong in our own strength, the very heart of which is utter helplessness, emptiness, and weakness.

When you worry, you are intruding into God's province. You are making yourself the father of the household instead of the child. You are setting yourself up as the master of God's kingdom instead of the servant for whom the Master provides.

The basis of prayer is man's need and God's ability to meet that need. When you really pray, you are confessing your utter helplessness. You are casting yourself completely and wholly upon God. You are delighting yourself in the Lord. Consequently, the Lord grants you the desires of your heart.

Our needs are manifold. Our perplexities are multifarious and variegated. Don't worry. Instead, turn your care into a prayer. Follow the example of Paul, who said, "I conferred not with flesh and blood" (Galatians 1:16). Conferring with flesh and blood about your worries instead of taking them to God is a fruitful cause for increased worry.

The woman who found her weakness—
and God's victory

Years ago, while I was still in the pastorate, I concluded a Sunday night service with the benediction. Even before the choir's response had ended, an anxious woman rushed up to me and asked if I would talk with her child, who was under the conviction of sin and wanted to be saved.

It was my joy to see that keen and energetic youngster enter into peace with God through Christ. We spent time in prayer together. As I rose to dismiss them, I realized that the mother was in agony, and she looked at me as if to say, "I am in such trouble. Can you help me?"

I asked her if she would like to speak with me. She grabbed the opportunity as a drowning man would grab a life vest. I asked the youngster to step into the next office for just a moment. Turning to the mother I said, "All right. Would you like to share with me the problem that is causing you this grief?"

She burst into uncontrollable sobs.

I assured her that having been pastor of a church of over 3,000 members for several years I was now shockproof. I further reminded her that everything would be held in strictest confidence.

Let me stop here long enough to tell you that this lady was one of the outstanding members of the church. She taught a Sunday school class, and was prominent in the Training Union and in the Women's Missionary Society. She almost never missed a service. She tithed her money. She knew her Bible. If Gallup had taken a poll of the membership, I am sure this lady would have ranked among the most respected of all members.

Finally, she blurted out her story. I sat transfixed with astonishment as she told the most sordid story of duplicity and sin I had ever heard from a supposedly respectable woman. At the end she nearly screamed out, "Preacher, have I committed the unpardonable sin?"

It was my joy to assure her from God's Word that if she still desired to repent, God would receive her. I assured her in the words of Jesus, who said, "Him that cometh to me I will in no wise cast out" (John 6:37).

For 11 years this woman had been trying to win, in her own strength, the battle of life. Though not yet 40 she had already aged considerably. Her health was poor. She was under psychiatric care. Finally she came to Christ and became a charming, radiant Christian. Her health returned, and her mind lost its shackles of life-destroying worry.

It wasn't until she confessed her helplessness and cast herself wholly upon God that she received strength to live dynamically. Afterward, as a child of God, she had a prayer life by which she maintained communion with God and kept unclogged the channel through which His strength could be released to her moment by moment and day by day.

23

WIN OVER WORRY
by Starting the Day Right

Starting your day with prayer will strengthen your poise.

Recall the story of Daniel. He had been hounded by men who were bent upon his destruction. Nevertheless, he did not alter his habit one iota. There was no ruffling of his spirit. He continued to make his prayer unto God three times a day. He prayed in a spirit of deep humility, recognizing his absolute dependence upon God.

Was this a sign of weakness? No! It was a sign of strength. To be sure, Daniel put his face in the dust before God, but he did not lose his courage before the wrath of King Darius. He sobbed like a heart-broken child when he knelt before his God, but he faced without a quiver the jaws of the hungry lions. What poise!

Prayer makes you efficient. This fact ought also to induce a greater interest in prayer. Martin Luther was not talking through his hat when he said, "I have so much business I cannot get along without spending three hours daily in prayer."

The benefits of prayer

What exactly does prayer do?

1. *Prayer saves you time.*

Prayer saves time by conditioning you for the day's activities and personal contacts. It saves time by conditioning those with whom you will associate. It saves time in that it makes available to you wisdom, which, in turn, leads to quick and proper decisions. "If any of you lack wisdom, let him ask of God, that giveth to all men liberally, and upbraideth not; and it shall be given him" (James 1:5).

This of course leads to peace of mind. Many people fret and mope around, wasting precious time simply because they don't know what to do or how to do it. The Lord has promised them the needed wisdom, but they either refuse it or neglect to avail themselves of it. The resultant loss of peace and time is incalculable.

How ridiculous it is for the Christian to ask for wisdom, and then immediately terminate his prayer. What would you think of a man who walked into your home and with apparent earnestness asked you a question, but then turned around and walked out before you had time to answer it? Remember, prayer is not a one-way street. It is a two-way street.

2. *Prayer puts you in touch with infinite intelligence.*

Prayer dispels the fogs of human ignorance. It banishes the darkness of self-destructive errors in judgment. People of prayer, even if they have academic limitations, are the recipients of a proper perspective and a keen understanding imparted to them by Him who is the Truth.

3. *Prayer makes grace available to you.*

Prayer provides the grace necessary to block out negative thoughts, distracting attitudes, and worries that torture the mind and damage the body. Prayer helps us with "casting down imaginations, and every high thing that exalteth itself against the knowledge of God, and bringing into captivity every thought to the obedience of Christ"

(2 Corinthians 10:5). When your thoughts are Christ's, they are not worry thoughts.

4. Prayer enlists divine strength.

Prayer enables you to effect the proper execution of your God-given responsibilities. While in the flesh upon this earth, our Lord prayed before every great endeavor.

5. Prayer can change negative circumstances.

Prayer can lead to the correction of circumstances that both consume time and saddle you with destructive grief. Do you remember the prayer of Moses and Aaron on behalf of their sister Miriam, who was suffering with leprosy? (see Numbers 12). How would that story have ended had it not been for their prayer?

6. Prayer leads to harmony.

Read once again the first chapters of the books of Acts. How differently history would have been written had it not been for the prayer of the 120 people in the upper room. The harmony that prevailed among them was one of the by-products of their prayer lives. We read concerning them, "All that believed were together, and had all things common" (Acts 2:44). Worry cannot survive in an atmosphere of such harmony.

7. Prayer produces faith.

And faith, of course, is the antidote to worry.

Faith is acting in confidence upon the word of another. The one who is faithful in his prayer life acts in confidence upon God's Word. He goes to God with all his dilemmas, all his assets, and all his liabilities. He acts in confidence upon God's Word, which tells him that if he delights himself in the Lord, the Lord will give him the desires of his heart. He prays, and God answers his prayers.

And God's answer is productive of greater faith—of a more eager and a more earnest disposition to act in confidence upon God's Word.

8. Prayer leads to inner security.

The person who spends time in regular prayer comes to know in his inmost soul that God's Word is true when He assures us, "I will never leave thee, nor forsake thee" (Hebrews 13:5). The resulting inner assurance leads to much greater efficiency. For instance, I know a man who always insisted on picking up the tab at the restaurant every time he and his friends were eating out. If he went to a ball game with others, he insisted on paying the bill. He constantly gave away expensive gifts— gifts he simply could not afford. Why? His dreadful insecurity is the only answer I can conceive. He compensated for his lack of inner security by trying to secure the friendship of a host of people whose gracious responses to his generosity gave him a temporary sense of well-being.

Enlisting the power of God's Spirit

When a man is properly related to God, he has within himself all the ingredients necessary to provide security, joy, and peace, regardless of his external conditions. This relationship is maintained only as a man spends time regularly with God.

Why pray? Because prayer is the means whereby you permit and invite God to so energize you that you live victoriously and overcome the world, the flesh, and the devil. Through prayer, you enlist the power of the Spirit of God to conquer the weaknesses of the flesh, including worry.

When your day starts with prayer, your thoughts are Christ's, they are not worry thoughts.

24

WIN OVER WORRY
by Knowing How to Ask

O n the basis of the teaching in Philippians 4:6, it would be well for us to ponder the elements of effectual praying.

To conquer worry, pray intelligently

"Let your requests be made known unto God."

A certain man spent six hours in prayer each day. To prevent himself from falling asleep, he would stand up and lean against a rope. If he fell asleep, he would fall.

What sort of prayer did he speak? He kept on repeating, "There is no God, but God. There is no God, but God." He repeated the same thing over and over again. He did not plead with God to give him anything; he simply repeated the words like a mantra.

In spite of his dedication, that was not prayer. If you get on your knees and simply repeat a certain formula, you are only speaking words. You are not praying.

Protestants have sometimes criticized Christians from other traditions for using written books or prayers or rosaries. But there are many Protestants who have reduced prayer to something entirely formulaic. They say prayers as did the farmer who each night prayed, "O Lord, bless me, my wife, my son John, his wife, us four, no more. Amen."

God does not hear you for your much speaking.

On Mount Carmel the wild-eyed prophets of Baal cut their flesh and chanted repetitiously, "O Baal, hear us!" They were not praying. The Bible tells us to make our requests known to God.

So get alone with God and tell Him what you want. Pour out your heart before Him. He does not care for high-flown language. Study the prayers of the Bible and you will be impressed by their unadorned directness. People simply spoke to God. So go to God as you go to your mother, your father, or your friend.

And don't assume God will dissipate your worries just because you get on your knees for a spell every morning and night. Pray intelligently. Tell God your problem. Tell Him that you have sinned, that you have worried. Tell Him that you want victory over it.

To conquer worry, pray definitely

Indefinite prayer is usually halfhearted, insincere praying.

There is no burden, no urgency, no overwhelming constraint in indefinite prayer. Indefinite prayer shows that you are not sure of the will of God. Therefore you know not what to pray for. Such prayer often indicates that you are trusting in the act of prayer rather than in the God who answers prayer.

Our minds are so constituted that we cannot fasten our desires intensely upon several things at the same time. Jesus said, "What things soever ye desire, when ye pray, believe that ye receive them, and ye shall have them" (Mark 11:24). Note that it is impossible to desire strongly that which is not definite.

Your problem is worry. Pray definitely about this problem. Pray definitely that God will give you victory over your distrust of Him. Pray that God will forgive you for intruding into His province by trying to carry on His business in your own power. Ask Him for the grace to cast all your cares upon Him.

In addition to all this, pray specifically concerning the problems causing your anxiety. If it is a wayward child, pray definitely and specifically for God's will to be done in his life and for God to give you the grace in the meantime to live triumphantly.

If it is financial difficulty, pray definitely that God will show you if you have been unwise in the handling of your money. If you have been unwise, ask Him to forgive you. Pray definitely that He will give you wisdom and grace to do what you can. Pray that He will miraculously do what you can't do. Then rest in the truth of Psalm 37:25: "I have been young, and now am old; yet have I not seen the righteous forsaken, nor his seed begging bread."

If you are suffering from a nervous stomach, pray definitely about it. Don't simply say, "Lord, take away my nervous stomach." Find out the causes of your condition. Be specific. Be definite. And then let your request be made known unto God. Or, as we could correctly translate it, "Make known your demands."

Every now and then I hear people say, "God heard my prayer, but He answered it a little differently than I was expecting."

But God gives definite answers to definite prayers.

Imagine if I had five sons and I prayed, "Lord, save my five sons." A few days later my neighbor's five sons all go to church and profess faith in Jesus Christ. Suppose that I then said, "Praise God; He answered my prayer. I prayed for the salvation of my five sons and He answered my prayer. He saved the five sons of my next-door neighbor." That is nonsense.

When you pray definitely, you can expect a definite answer. Pray for bread. God will give you bread, not a stone. Pray for fish. God will give you a fish, not a serpent (see Matthew 7:9-11).

To conquer worry, pray persistently

Don't be afraid to make demands of God. You can make demands because of your relationship with God through Christ: "My God shall supply all your need according to his riches in glory by Christ Jesus" (Philippians 4:19).

God has promised to supply all your needs. You can demand the fulfillment of that promise—with this warning, however. You are not to say, "Lord, supply all of my needs." Rather, you are to specifically and definitely make known those needs one by one. And then pray persistently. Your cares are persistent. Therefore, make your prayers persistent.

Pray to God and then pray again. If the Lord does not answer you the first time, be grateful that you have good reason for praying again. If He does not answer your requests the second time, thank Him that He loves you so much that He wants to hear your voice again. If He keeps you waiting until you have gone to Him seven times, say to yourself, "Now I know that I worship the God of Elijah, for Elijah's God let him go again seven times before the blessing was given."

Count it an honor to be permitted to wrestle in prayer even as Jacob wrestled with the angel during the long watches of the night. This is the way God develops His servants. Jacob never would have been renamed *Israel* had he not wrestled for the blessing from the angel. He kept on wrestling until he prevailed. Then he became a prince of God. Worry cannot exist with determined prayer.

In the Gospels, Jesus taught us to pray. In doing so, He gave two great illustrations, which are recorded in the eleventh and in the eighteenth chapters of Luke.

In Luke 11, we read of a man who wanted to borrow bread at midnight. This man is a striking example of the kind of spirit Jesus desires for us to inculcate. The borrower was in dire need. He was terribly in earnest and would not take no for an answer (verse 8).

Jesus said that when you pray, you should be just as earnest and persistent as this man was. You need the blessing of God much more than he needed three loaves of bread. You are seeking something that means more than bread, and just as the importunity of the borrower finally wins out, so the soul set upon finding God will command His attention and be heard.

God has no time for lukewarm pleas, for easygoing, halfhearted prayers. If the sense of need is not great, if you forget about the matter before the day is over, God will pay little heed to your prayer. If you have something vital at issue, if you are willing to give time and effort, and if you press your claim home to a finish, God will listen.

The man who is willing to quit, or who can quit, is not in the condition of mind and heart to appreciate the favor of God. The soul who counts it the biggest privilege on earth to know God, who seeks for Him and His blessings as men seek for silver and gold, will not only be rewarded, but also will be conditioned to estimate rightly what has been received.

Jesus then said, "I say unto you, Ask, and it shall be given you; seek, and ye shall find; knock, and it shall be opened unto you. For every one that asketh receiveth; and he that seeketh findeth; and to him that knocketh it shall be opened" (Luke 11:9-10).

This is not the easy passage some people think it is. It does not mean that all you have to do is ask for something and you will receive it, or knock and the door will fly open. Jesus was referring to a life that is one continual search after God, a constant seeking, a daily asking, a habitual knocking.

This is the only antidote to worry, which itself can be perpetual. Let your prayer be perpetual. It means that you must desire that which lies behind the closed door intensely enough to knock with unshaken persistence. Jesus was saying that to such knocking the door will open. To seeking of that sort will come the answer that makes life full and rich.

The parable found in the eighteenth chapter of Luke is even more striking, as it represents a case where the delayed answer is misunderstood. The petitioner is presented in the figure of a poor widow seeking vindication and protection from an unjust judge. The judge is the perfect embodiment of heartless wickedness. No more complete portrait of depravity was ever drawn than that which appears in this terse phrase: "which feared not God, neither regarded man" (Luke 18:2).

The feeble, insignificant petitioner was scorned. No heed was given. But Jesus said she continued to press her plea for justice until, in absolute selfishness and for no other reason, the judge granted the request: "Though I fear not God, nor regard man; yet because this widow troubleth me, I will avenge her, lest by her continual coming she weary me" (Luke 18:4-5).

The argument is this: If a man like that can be moved to do what means nothing to him, will not God hear the continual cry of His people, whom He loves with a boundless compassion? We will endure long periods when prayers seem unanswered. We will experience long days of darkness, sometimes years of wearisome waiting, while countless petitions are sent to a heaven that seems deaf and empty. This is the time about which Jesus speaks. He says, "Cry on; God will hear. He is not heartless, neither has He forgotten."

This parable is for the time when faith has staggered and the heart has grown sick with waiting. Let us remember that the longest delay to us may be as the twinkling of an eye to the plans of God. Preacher Alexander Maclaren said years ago, "Heaven's clock does not beat in the same note with our little chronometers."

Jesus teaches us to pray on. He says we must not quit. We must not doubt. God knows when to answer. He knows the best time and the most fitting place. We can, in all confidence, leave the question of when and where to Him. Of one thing we may be sure: He will answer. Worthy prayer does not become discouraged. It does not surrender. This is the power that defeats worry.

To conquer worry, pray in faith

Faith is acting in confidence upon the word of another. Faith in God is acting in confidence upon His Word. You were saved that way. It is also in this way you become mighty with God.

You develop faith as you meditate upon God's Word, the Bible. "So then faith cometh by hearing, and hearing by the word of God" (Romans 10:17). Prayer and the Word of God are inseparably connected. "Feasting" on the Word of God is productive of that faith without which prayer is useless.

Through the Word of God the Lord speaks to our hearts and conditions our hearts for prayer. In prayer we speak to Him in faith. So many times in the Scriptures we have passages indicating that the Lord spoke first, after which the one who heard the Word of the Lord spoke to Him in prayer. For example:

> The word of the LORD came unto me, saying, Before I formed thee in the belly I knew thee; and before thou camest forth out of the womb I sanctified thee, and I ordained thee a prophet unto the nations. Then said I, Ah, Lord GOD! Behold, I cannot speak: for I am a child (Jeremiah 1:4-6).

You remember also Daniel's great prayer. In the first year of the reign of King Darius we see Daniel reading the Word of God. He had in his hand the prophecy of Jeremiah, in which the Lord had promised that the desolation of Jerusalem would last 70 years. After reading this prophetic promise, Daniel turned to the Lord. The reading of the Word of God led to prayer. The reading of God's Word was productive of the faith that made prayer effectual.

The German theologian J.A. Bengel had the reputation of knowing the secret of effectual prayer. One day a fellow believer watched him at the close of the day. He saw the old saint sitting before a large Bible, reading slowly, often stopping and meditating, with silent tears running down his cheeks. After reading and meditating a long time, Bengel closed the book and began to speak to God in prayer. His heart had been prepared through the reading of the Word. Neglect of the daily reading of the Word of God and meditation on it soon results in neglected prayer as well.

The secret to earnest and effectual prayer—the prayer of faith—is faithful and diligent study of the Scriptures. Faith is essential to effectual prayer. All real prayer has, as its basis, a firm faith in a God who responds to the quest of the human soul. But without faith it is impossible to please Him:

He that cometh to God must believe that he is, and that
he is a rewarder of them that diligently seek him (Hebrews
11:6).

We come to God by our hearts and not by our intellects.

The first condition of entering into His fellowship is a faith not only
that God is, but also that He will be found by the soul who honestly
and persistently seeks for Him. God is not found by those who look
for Him in the spirit of cold curiosity. He is not found by those who
simply desire to extend the range of their intellectual conquest. This
is the reason many self-styled philosophers and pseudoscientists have
been unable to come to any clear conception of God. It was to men of
this type that Zophar said, "Canst thou by searching find out God?
Canst thou find out the Almighty unto perfection?" (Job 11:7).

When a man says in the pride of his intellect, "I will now see if
there be any God," he may turn his telescope upon the farthest heavens
and count the myriad worlds that wander in the blue abyss. He may
peer among the atoms and divide and subdivide the electrons, but the
greatest thing in the universe will still be hidden from his eyes.

The laws of logic, the theories of philosophy, and the investigations
of chemistry and physics all have their place and are of great value, but
they are not milestones on the road to fellowship with God.

The man who can say with the Hebrew psalmist, "My soul thirst-
eth for God, for the living God: when shall I come and appear before
God?" (Psalm 42:2) is more nearly on the road to His presence. The
humble man who with simple and sincere faith reaches out after God
will find Him while the philosopher is groping in the shadows of theory
and the scientist is bewildered by the results of experiments.

If you want to enter into the prayer life that conquers care, spend
some time each day with the Word of God. The time you spend will
be productive of faith that pleases God. This time will condition you
for communion with God, and as you commune with God you will

develop ever more confidence in God, and this glorious cycle will continue unabated for as long as you live.

To conquer worry, pray privately

> When thou prayest, enter into thy closet, and when thou
> has shut thy door, pray to thy Father which is in secret; and
> thy Father which seeth in secret shall reward thee openly
> (Matthew 6:6).

God deals with us face to face and heart to heart. You cannot have audience with a king and be engaged with the crowd at the same time. The matters between you and God are too sacred and personal to be laid bare to the eyes of the crowd.

Furthermore, prayer calls for such concentration, such focus, such rallying of powers that it demands the quiet of the private space. When we pray, we are going to share with God things that are intensely personal—secrets of the heart, sins that need to be confessed, yearnings deepest in the soul that need to be whispered into His ear. Also, we must give God the opportunity to speak to us. God's "still small voice" cannot be heard in the clamor of day-to-day living.

Jesus did not mean that no one could pray except within an empty room. He did mean that the doors of the heart and mind must be shut to the world. When you have shut these doors, then you have the space to pray. For in prayer, nobody is present but ourselves and God. Even our dearest friend is outside those doors. He or she may be in the same room physically, or sitting on the same pew, but he or she is still outside. We must not allow any distraction. There should be a mental sign placed outside ourselves that says,

> Engaged in important business with the Almighty. Keep
> out!

I tell you: Worry cannot abide when you are locked up with God in the secret sanctuary of prayer.

To conquer worry, pray thankfully

The kind of prayer that kills worry is the kind that asks cheerfully and joyfully. Pray, "Lord, I am in financial straits. I bless Thee for this condition, and I ask Thee to supply all my needs."

Pray, "Lord I am sick. I thank Thee for this affliction, for Thou hast promised that all things work together for good to those who love the Lord. Now hear me, I beseech Thee—if it please Thee."

Or pray, "Lord I am in great trouble. I thank Thee for this trouble for I know that it contains a blessing even though the envelope is black-edged. Now, Lord, give me grace as I pass though this trouble."

This is the kind of prayer that kills worry.

25

WIN OVER WORRY
by Living Close to God

The story is told of two Irishmen, Pat and Mike, who had narrowly escaped death on a sinking ship. They were floundering around in icy ocean waters on a couple of planks. Pat was addicted to the grossest profanity but was willing to repent of it if the Lord would come to his rescue. Mike thought this theology sound. And so Pat assumed a pious countenance and began to pray.

Just before Pat arrived at the main thesis of his repentant prayer, Mike spotted a ship coming toward them. As delighted as Columbus when he first spotted the shores of the New World, Mike hollered, "Hold it, Pat. Don't commit yerself. Here's a ship." And Pat immediately stopped praying.

Isn't that the way many of us are?

Too often, the only time we pray is when we are in a jam. And as soon as things improve, we forget God. Our model verse is Psalm 50:15: "Call upon me in the day of trouble: I will deliver thee, and thou shalt glorify me."

Spiritually speaking, most of us can much better afford adversity than prosperity. Like the Israelites of old, it seems that when our prosperity expands, our spirituality contracts. Like Pat, we call upon the

Lord only when things are going wrong. But as soon as conditions improve, we resort to our own resources. The Lord is an escape hatch—nothing more.

Maintaining a spirit of prayer

The tense used in the Greek text of Philippians 4:6 is present imperative. It carries the idea of ongoing action. In effect, Paul was saying, "Don't perpetually worry. Perpetually pray." Let perpetual prayer take the place of perpetual concern.

Our little son Johnny breathed only once every two-and-a-half minutes for the first three hours he was in this world. Because of his deficient breathing, inadequate supplies of oxygen reached his brain, with the result that brain tissues were destroyed and body movement was impaired.

Many Christians are suffering from the spiritual equivalent of this condition. Prayer is the Christian's breath. When breathing is obstructed, health is jeopardized. When the Christian permits an obstruction in his or her prayer life, spiritual health declines. An inadequate supply of the oxygen of prayer destroys spiritual fiber and impairs Christian effectiveness. If we want to be spiritually healthy, we must pray ceaselessly. As the Word says, "Pray without ceasing" (1 Thessalonians 5:17).

The Christian's prayer life should be one of incessant prayer, "praying always," as Paul said in Ephesians 6:18. This means praying in all seasons and on all occasions. If you want to conquer worry, you must always maintain a spirit of prayer. You must live in a prayerful disposition.

Can we really pray ceaselessly?

One of my theology professors, while discussing the meaning of "pray without ceasing," recalled the experience of some ministers he knew. They had congregated early and were waiting for the Monday morning ministers' meeting. As they talked in the vestibule, this verse was mentioned. Discussion became spirited. It wasn't long until they readily agreed that the verse puzzled them. How could one possibly pray without ceasing?

It so happened that a cleaning woman overheard them, and at this point she joined in.

"I always pray," she told them. "When I go to bed at night, I thank the Lord for the joy of resting on His everlasting arms. When I awaken the next morning, I ask Him to open my eyes that I may behold new and wondrous things out of His Word. When I bathe, I ask Him to cleanse me from secret faults. When I dress, I ask Him to clothe me with humility and love for souls. When I eat, I ask Him to cause me to grow on the bread of His Word..."

She continued like this for several minutes, and taught those professional ministers a lesson they never forgot.

Praying without ceasing means keeping your mind attuned with Christ and attuned to the will of God. Though you might not be involved in deliberate and conscious contact with God, you *are* aware of His presence and of the fact that your life is being regulated by His will. It is much the same as a mother who is attuned to the needs and wants of her infant, even while she is sleeping—for the slightest whimper will awaken her. Likewise, the slightest prompting of the Spirit should immediately get our attention.

Isaiah wrote, "Thou wilt keep him in perfect peace, whose mind is stayed on thee: because he trusteth in thee" (Isaiah 26:3). Being attuned to God keeps you in the awareness of His presence. And this produces perfect peace. Prayer is thus an essential ingredient of the peaceful lifestyle.

The pages of the Bible are full of the names of men and women who prayed. All those who had power with God were people of prayer. How else would we explain the poise of Deborah, Daniel, or Hannah?

The great example, of course, is our Lord, whose whole life was a prayer. Before He did anything, He prayed. After He did anything, He prayed. He prayed morning, noon, and night. Sometimes He prayed all night. Whenever He was alone He prayed. Prayer was never off

His lips and never out of His heart. He was the perfect example of unceasing prayer.

One word of caution.

There are those who excuse their lack of a quiet time with God by saying, "I pray all the time. I pray while I am driving the car to work. I pray when I go about my business. I pray all the time, in whatever I do." Now this is all well and good. But it is essential also to spend a set period apart with God each day. You need to be alone with God for at least some of the time, just as you need to be alone with a husband or wife.

Prayer in practice

Charles Simeon devoted four hours each morning to prayer. Charles Wesley spent two hours daily in prayer. It is said that John Fletcher stained the walls of his room with the breath of his prayers. Sometimes he would pray all night. He said, "I would not rise from my seat without lifting my heart to God." Prayer is the powerhouse of your spiritual life. Not surprisingly, Adoniram Judson gave this advice: "Make all practical sacrifices to maintain it."

You may not have hours at a stretch to devote to prayer. That is fine. D.L. Moody never spent more than 15 minutes in any one prayer. But he prayed often and about everything.

As far as is possible, then, ensure that you have time set aside, preferably at the same time each day, to commune with God. Fifteen minutes for prayer and 15 minutes for Bible study may be enough, though more is always recommended. Personally I find the morning the best time. The more I commit myself to the Lord in the morning, the less I have to confess at night. The morning quiet time is like a spiritual breakfast:

> It is written, Man shall not live by bread alone, but by every word that proceedeth out of the mouth of God (Matthew 4:4).

> As newborn babes, desire the sincere milk of the word, that ye may grow (1 Peter 2:2).

If you want to be strong, you must have spiritual food at the beginning of the day to sustain you through it. You are not likely to suffer great temptations while you are sleeping. But great strains and stresses will be encountered during the day. Another old professor of mine had a motto: "No Bible, no breakfast. Speak to no one until you have spoken to God."

The effectiveness of your brief moments of prayer during the day will be contingent on these longer periods spent with God as the day begins. Don't pretend you have no time. Some people have more money than others. Some have more talent. But we are all on the same level when it comes to time. We each have 60 minutes in each hour and 24 hours in each day. How we organize them is up to us.

As an evangelist I was away from home a lot. On a few occasions on my way from one city to another, I was able to stop at home for a few minutes. Being able to do so delighted my heart, and my wife and son gave evidence that this delight was reciprocated.

Suppose, however, that when I had a week off between meetings, I refused to go home. Suppose I used that time to visit some friends instead. The next time I "bounced in" at home I would probably have been "bounced out" just as fast. But my family knew that I loved to be at home and that I spent every possible moment there. That made the briefest of visits a pleasure for all of us.

So too our brief visits with the Lord bring mutual rejoicing if we are faithful in setting aside larger segments of time to commune with Him in deliberate and earnest intercession.

Finally

When you find yourself worrying, utilize this formula of praise, poise, and prayer, and God will give you peace. Also, when you pray, you will be given strength to offer praise and to manifest poise. As you pray, you will become effective in prayer.

Now believe this: Believe that God will give you precisely what He has promised to give you if you will meet the conditions. He will give you peace. He cannot go back on His promise. He is the God "that cannot lie" (Titus 1:2).

Are you one who prays, but only says words? While you are asking God to give you victory over worry, are you at the very same time worrying that you are not praying correctly? Are you worrying that maybe you have not met all of the conditions?

Stop psychoanalyzing yourself! Don't be a spiritual hypochondriac. Get your mind off yourself and onto God. Spend enough time in your prayer thanking God for what He has done and praising Him for who He is. Then you will be conditioned to pray intelligently, definitely, persistently, and in faith.

As you pray, picture yourself a perfectly adjusted, dynamic, radiant personality living in the strength of God and to the glory of God. This is certainly God's will for you. By faith, then, take God at His Word, and lay hold upon Him in prayer, and you will bring glory to Him and experience peace in your mind.

You are what you think you are. Stop, therefore, insulting God. Recognize yourself as a redeemed soul. You are a child of the King. You are in league with the Creator of the universe. Recognize yourself as a potential recipient of qualities, attitudes, and resources that will glorify God and bless those around you as you live triumphantly over every worry and care.

PART 3

WHAT YOU CAN WIN

26

PEACE IN PLACE
OF WORRY

I n Philippians 4:6, the apostle Paul tells us to pray, which helps us to conquer worry. Then he adds:

> And the peace of God, which passeth all understanding, shall keep your hearts and minds through Christ Jesus (Philippians 4:7).

The word translated "peace" can also be translated "tranquility," "harmony," "concord," "security," "safety," "prosperity," and "felicity."

Worry cannot survive in this kind of atmosphere. Just as worry involves "dividing the mind," so peace involves "uniting the mind"—fastening it upon worthwhile goals and stimulating it with worthwhile motives.

God is the Author of this peace. It is "the peace of God." And God does not confuse us. "For God is not the author of confusion, but of peace, as in all churches of the saints" (1 Corinthians 14:33). And in the Word of God peace and unity go together, for Christians are to endeavor "to keep the unity of the Spirit in the bond of peace" (Ephesians 4:3).

This is a genuine peace begotten of God.

This peace is not possessed by the hedonist. Such a person takes everything lightly—snaps his fingers, whistles, and sings. This fellow is a heedless, foolish, light-headed, and light-heeled person who, for a little while, may dance and sing. He simply postpones his sorrow. The day will come when he will give an account. That day will come swiftly and with a vengeance.

This peace is not possessed by the stoic. The stoic braces his nerves. He will be shaken and moved by nothing. Run a knife into him and he will feel the pain, but he will not show it. Despite all manner of knocks and blows in the rough-and-tumble world, he has set his face to the wind and will endure without complaining. This may be commendable, but it is not peace.

This peace is not possessed by the epicurean. The epicurean chortles out, "Let us eat, drink, and be merry, for tomorrow we die." These are not steel-nerved stoics. They live it up, but they know their long-term prospects are poor.

The peace of God is deep-seated and realistic. It is not a self-manufactured hallucination designed to color the facts. This peace is based upon the fact of God's all-sufficiency. It is also based upon our willingness to cast ourselves in self-confessed helplessness upon Him—in response to which He lives through us His own life, bringing harmony, purpose, meaning, and poise.

Peace with God, and the peace of God

The distinction between peace *with* God and the peace *of* God is important. "Being justified by faith, we have peace with God through our Lord Jesus Christ" (Romans 5:1). But not every child of God has the peace of God. No one can enjoy the peace of God who does not have peace with God. On the other hand, it is possible, as witnessed by the experience of multitudes of Christians, to have peace with God and fail to appropriate the peace of God.

This peace of God has its foundation in the fact that God does all things well. It has its source in the fact that Jesus "will never leave thee, nor forsake thee" (Hebrews 13:5).

Do you remember the story in Mark 4 of our Lord's trip across the Sea of Galilee? He was asleep in the bottom of the boat. The winds became furious. The waves sprang higher and higher into the air. Soon a tempestuous storm was raging. The little boat was perched perilously aloft a crest one moment only to be dashed into the vortex the next. The terrified disciples cried out, "Lord, save us. We perish!" Yet Jesus was asleep! What peace.

When Jesus arose and subdued the storm, He turned to the disciples and said, "Why are ye so fearful? How is it that ye have no faith?" I can hear them muttering, "Little faith? Little faith? We are veteran seamen. We have never seen a storm like this, and You call it little faith!" But Jesus hadn't said, "Let us go out to the middle of the sea and get drowned." He had said, "Let us pass over unto the other side" (Mark 4:35).

Now, when you have invited Christ into your life and you have turned the helm over to His control and you have heard His words of assurance, "I will never leave thee, nor forsake thee" (Hebrews 13:5), then there is made available to you a peace the world cannot give and cannot take away.

The peace of God, the Bible says, is beyond understanding (Philippians 4:7). This may be interpreted in two ways.

First, it may be interpreted as meaning that God's peace is beyond the scope of human comprehension. It is deeper, broader, sweeter, and more heavenly than the joyful Christian himself can explain. He enjoys what he cannot understand.

Second, it may be interpreted as meaning that God's peace exceeds in effectiveness any mere human means of reducing stress.

Imagine a man who worries. He tries, through the efforts of his own understanding, to resolve his worries. He fails—miserably. He may resort to stoicism or epicureanism or the power of positive thinking, but no matter what he does, he fails.

This man comes to God's Word. He responds affirmatively to God's commands. Having entered into peace with God, he now utilizes the formula that gives the peace of God: praise plus poise plus prayer. Perfect peace is now his privileged possession. In this sense, God's peace surpasses understanding in that it far exceeds in effectiveness any attempted solution devised by human science.

The peace of God is indestructible

God's peace "shall keep your hearts and minds through Christ Jesus" (Philippians 4:7). Paul here brings into union the conceptions of peace and of war, for he employs a distinctly military word to express the office of this divine peace. That word, translated "shall keep," is the same word used in another of his letters and translated "kept... with a garrison" (2 Corinthians 11:32).

This peace of God takes upon itself military functions. It garrisons the heart and mind. The peace of God garrisons and guards the whole person in the full scope of that person's thinking, feeling, willing, desiring, and acting. This divine peace can be enjoyed even in the midst of conflict. It can guard you against all care, anxiety, change, suffering, and misfortune. It gives unalterable rest in God.

Deep in the bosom of the ocean, beneath the region where winds howl and billows break, there is calm, but the calm is not stagnation. Each drop in the fathomless abyss is eventually raised to the surface by the power of sunbeams, expanded there by heat, and sent on some beneficent mission across the world. Even so, deep in our hearts—beneath the storm, beneath the raging winds and the lashing waves—this peace forms a central, life-sustaining, and refreshing calm.

Drops of this calm may be raised to the surface of our behavior by the power of the Son of Righteousness—Jesus Christ, the Light of the World—and expanded there by the heat of the Holy Spirit and sent on beneficent service across the world.

The peace of God is perpetual

The tense of the phrase "shall keep" in the Greek text is future active indicative, and the context makes it clear that the peace of God will proceed in continuous and unabated action.

Stop perpetually worrying. Perpetually let your requests be made known unto God. And you will have the assurance that perpetual peace will garrison and guard your mind and heart through Christ Jesus. What an antidote to worry!

The assurance of this peace is conditional upon no outside circumstance, for this peace is possible only through Christ. A life without Christ is a life without peace. Without Him you may have excitement, worldly success, fulfilled dreams, fun, and gratified passions—but you will never have peace!

Horatio G. Spafford was a successful lawyer in Chicago and a member of the Fullerton Avenue Presbyterian Church in that city. In the financial crisis of 1873 he lost most of his property. In the stress and strain of the times, he prevailed on his wife and four daughters to take a trip to France to get as far away from the scene of worry as possible. He booked a passage for them on the *Ville du Havre.* They set sail November 15. For a week the trip was uneventful, and its hundreds of passengers were enjoying the restful bliss of an ocean voyage. That is, until the night of November 22.

Shortly after midnight the *Loch Earn,* bound for New York, collided with the *Ville du Havre.* Within a few minutes, the French ocean liner sank beneath the waves. The *Loch Earn,* which was not damaged by the collision, rescued as many survivors as could be found. Of the 226 passengers on the *Ville du Havre,* only 87 survived.

Mrs. Spafford was among the survivors, but the four daughters perished. As soon as Mrs. Spafford reached land, she telegraphed from France to her husband: "Saved alone. Children lost. What shall I do?"

The Chicago attorney left immediately to join his wife and bring her back to Chicago. It was in the depths of their bereavement that he wrote his one and only hymn, "It Is Well with My Soul." The grief of his terrible loss and the peace he experienced as he and his wife submitted their lives to God's providential dealings are described in the stanzas of the hymn:

When peace like a river attendeth my way,
When sorrows like sea billows roll;
Whatever my lot, Thou hast taught me to say,
"It is well, it is well with my soul."

Though Satan should buffet, tho' trials should come,
Let this blest assurance control,
That Christ has regarded my helpless estate,
And hath shed His own blood for my soul.

My sin, O, the bliss of this glorious thought,
My sin not in part but the whole,
Is nailed to the cross and I bear it no more,
Praise the Lord, praise the Lord, O my soul!

And Lord, haste the day when the faith shall be sight,
The clouds be rolled back as a scroll,
The trump shall resound and the Lord shall descend,
"Even so," it is well with my soul.

Christian friend, before you were saved you had no peace, did you? The Christless heart is like a troubled sea that cannot rest. There is no peace for it.

Now you are a Christian. The Lord has brought you peace with respect to your relationship with Him and with respect to your outlook on eternity. However, if you are to enjoy the peace of God over daily worries and cares and anxieties, small though they be—"the little foxes spoil the vines"—you must fix your mind upon Him, "looking unto Jesus" (Hebrews 12:2).

Keep your mind stayed on Him. This will enable you to fulfill the biblical formula of praise, poise, and prayer. Praise and poise and prayer together will bring you peace, in the grace of God. As Christ lives in you "your peace shall be as a river, and your righteousness as the waves of the sea" (see Isaiah 48:18).

27

CAN YOU HANDLE A LIFE
WITHOUT WORRY?

During my sophomore year in high school, my English teacher required the class to read the autobiography of Benjamin Franklin.

This book made an indelible impression upon me. Benjamin Franklin concluded that there were 13 areas of his life that he needed to master. He set his goal to do so in a disciplined and scheduled way. He laid out a grid with the 13 "virtues" listed in the left-hand column and the weeks 1–13 across the top. Each week he would major on one "virtue," while also grading himself on how well or how poorly he was doing with the other 12.

With this system, Franklin was able to cover all 13 "virtues" every three months. Toward the end of his life he said he had mastered each of the virtues except order and organization.

Using this book to change your life

A one-time read-through of this book will not correct a lifelong habit of worrying. If you're serious about winning over worry—turning a divided mind into a focused mind, learning how to manage stress—you must systematically, and with discipline, incorporate this book's principles into your daily life. Winning over worry isn't a magic spell.

Nor is it a quick fix. It is a skill you master by applying yourself consistently over a period of time.

Think how many times you fell before you mastered the skill of riding a bicycle. Reflect upon the numerous repetitions required in learning a second language. Consider the slow but steady progress that takes a musical novice to the point of becoming an accomplished musician.

To win over worry, you will need to repeat the behavior required for winning over worry until it no longer requires your conscious attention, but becomes the expression of your subconscious. You may even find it helpful to use Benjamin Franklin's method of keeping score.

It may be that you have no problem maintaining the habit of "rejoicing," but you spend very little time "counting your blessings." If so, then you will need to focus on improving in that area.

Whatever you decide to major on as you deal with worry, you can maximize the power of spaced repetition by writing this book's PEACE FORMULA on index cards and posting them around your home and workplace.

I prepared my initial lecture on this subject more than 55 years ago. I wrote the book more than 50 years ago. To this day I refer to it as one would refer to a manual. I commend the material in this book not because I wrote it, but simply because it contains what I have learned through Scripture, observation, and personal experience—and because it has worked for me and thousands of others.

Where to get further help

On the last page of this book, you stand at the beginning of a journey. It is a journey that can take you out of needless anxiety and into the fullness of living. If you would like further help or advice, or access to other materials that can help you on your way, I hope you will feel free to contact me.

I personally can be reached at the following address: John Edmund Haggai, P.O. Box 921311, Norcross, Georgia 30010-7311, U.S.A.

Peace be with you—and stay in touch!

INDEXES

GENERAL INDEX

SCRIPTURE INDEX

OTHER BOOKS BY
JOHN EDMUND HAGGAI

How to Win Over Pain
How to Win Over Fear
How to Win Over Loneliness
My Son Johnny
Lead On!
The Leading Edge
The Steward
Be Careful What You Call Impossible
The Wackersberg Connection
Paul J. Meyer and the Art of Giving
The Seven Secrets of Effective Business Relationships
Exponential
Influential Leadership

ABOUT THE AUTHOR

John Edmund Haggai

Founder and Chairman
Haggai Institute

John Edmund Haggai has been called a visionary, a Christian world states-man, and an evangelist and a master of the pulpit—all of which are true of this dynamic man of God.

Never content to follow the crowd, Dr. Haggai initiated a unique and for-ward-thinking mission plan in obedience to the Great Commission. A visit to Asia in the early 1960s convinced Haggai that changes in global geopolitics, brought about by the end of colonialism, required a new strategy for world evangelism. In 1969, after years of research, prayer, and development, he pre-sided over the first advanced leadership seminar designed to empower and mobilize nationals to reach their own people for Christ.

Haggai Institute has trained tens of thousands of Christian clergy and lay leaders working in almost all the non-Western countries of the world. They multiply their effectiveness significantly by passing on their training to an average of 100 other leaders each.

After more than 60 years in public service, this man shows no signs of slow-ing down in his work for the kingdom. He continues to lead the ministry, write his memoirs, and speak in churches, universities, seminaries, and busi-ness groups throughout the world.

Dr. Haggai, alumnus of Moody Bible Institute (where he was named "Alumnus of the Year") and Furman University, has garnered many awards and earned honorary doctorates from both sides of the Pacific.

He has authored more than a dozen books, including *How to Win Over Worry, My Son Johnny, Lead On!,* and *The Leading Edge.*

John Edmund Haggai was born in Louisville, Kentucky, the son of a Syrian immigrant and a New Englander whose English ancestors settled in America during the 1600s. John and his wife, Christine, live in Atlanta, Georgia; how-ever, their influence touches millions around the globe.